PLACES

*A Directory of Public Places for Private Events
& Private Places for Public Functions*

Scott Osman
Photographer

TENTH HOUSE ENTERPRISES, INC.   New York

PLACES: A DIRECTORY OF PUBLIC PLACES FOR PRIVATE EVENTS AND
PRIVATE PLACES FOR PUBLIC FUNCTIONS

Copyright © by Tenth House Enterprises, Inc. 1978, 1979, 1980/1981, 1982/1983

All Rights Reserved.
Fourth Edition

Library of Congress No.: 80-50723
ISBN: 0-9603310-2-6

Cover by D. Bruce Zahor

Production and typesetting by Gail Murray

No part of this book may be used or reproduced in any manner whatsoever without written permission. For information, address Tenth House Enterprises, Inc., Caller Box 810, Gracie Station, New York, N.Y. 10028.

To order a copy of **PLACES** send a check or money order for $16.95 which includes postage, tax and handling. Add $1.50 for first class or air mail.
Checks or money orders to be made out to Tenth House Enterprises, Inc., and mailed to:

Caller Box 810
Gracie Station
New York, N.Y. 10028

Printed in the United States of America

CONTENTS

	Page
Armories	5
Auditoriums (Seating 499 or less)	69
Auditoriums (Seating 500 or more)	6
Ballrooms	10
Bandshells	94
Block Parties	50
Boats, Barges & Balloons	12
Carousels	174
Children's Birthday Parties	174
Churches	19
Clock Towers	48
Colleges	117
Concert Spaces	88
Conference Centers	29
Conference Rooms	69
Dance Studio & Performance Spaces	95
Discos	35
Environmental Centers	39
Exhibitions/Expositions	42
Exhibits: Outdoors	49
Fairgrounds	50
Flea Markets	50
Gallery Spaces	49
Historic Houses	136
Hotels	53
Landmarks	136
Libraries	59
Lofts	65
Mansions	181
Meeting Rooms	69
Mini-Parks	85
Parks	83
Parties	136
Performance Spaces (Concert/Recital)	88
Performance Spaces (Dance/Theater)	95
Picnic Areas	83
Piers	110
Plazas	85
Poetry Reading Places	112
Private Parties/Private Places (in New York City)	136
Private Parties/Public Places (in New York City)	153
Private Parties/Private Places (near New York City)	149
Private Parties/Public Places (near New York City)	169
Private Party Places (Nationwide)	181
Public Schools	121
Recital Spaces	88
Rehearsal Spaces	114
Rinks	115
Schools	117
Screening Rooms	127
Stadiums	128
Steps	130
Street Fairs	50
Studio Space	131
Supper Clubs	35
Theaters	95
Universities	117
Wedding/Wedding Reception Places	136
Y's	133

Park Avenue Armory, Seventh Regiment

ARMORIES

Requests for non-military use of State Armories should be directed to the individual Armory Officers in Charge and Control. Requests should be on the business or official letterhead of requesting organization or agency and should contain the following information:

Name and address of organization, agency or individual of the prospective lessee; the purpose, character and extent of the use; commercial, non-profit, charitable, governmental or youth activity; space to be used; day and hours of use, including moving in and out; admission charge, if any

Manhattan:	125 West 14th Street New York, N.Y. 10011	691-0710
	68 Lexington Avenue New York, N.Y. 10010	532-6969
	643 Park Avenue New York, N.Y. 10021	288-0200
	2366 Fifth Avenue New York, N.Y. 10037	926-5800
	216 Fort Washington Avenue New York, N.Y. 10032	923-5580
Bronx:	1122 Franklin Avenue Bronx, N.Y. 10456	542-1122
	29 West Kingsbridge Road Bronx, N.Y. 10456	584-5700
Brooklyn:	1322 Bedford Avenue Brooklyn, N.Y. 11216	622-7500
	1579 Bedford Avenue Brooklyn, N.Y. 11225	467-5400
	1402 Eighth Avenue Brooklyn, N.Y. 11215	788-3537
	355 Marcy Avenue Brooklyn, N.Y. 11206	387-9102
Queens:	9305 - 168th Street Jamaica, N.Y. 11433	739-0421
Richmond:	321 Manor Road Staten Island, N.Y. 10314	442-8400

* * * * * * *

AUDITORIUMS

(Seating 500 or more)

Venue	Seats
Brooklyn Academy of Music/Lepercq Space	500
C.W. Post Center of Long Island University	500
Columbia University/St. Paul's Chapel	500
Diplomat Hotel/Crystal Room	500
District 1199	500
Edison Theater	500
Educational Alliance	500
Holiday Inn (at the Coliseum)	500
James Weldon Johnson Community Center, Inc. (outdoor theater)	500
La Guardia Memorial House	500
Marc Ballroom	500
New York City Mission Society	500
People's Institutional A.M.E. Church	500
Queens College/QC Theatre	500
Reformed Church of Staten Island	500
St. Hilda's and St. Hugh's School	500
St. Mark's Church in-the-Bowery	500
St. Peter's Church	500
Staten Island Academy (gymnasium)	500
Universalist Church	500
Brooklyn College/Gershwin Hall	504
Barbizon Plaza Hotel	505
Wagner Junior High School	512
Long Island University — Brooklyn	550
Congregation B'nai Jeshurun	600
Flushing Jewish Center	600
Brooklyn YWCA	605
Queens College Student Union	605
Roberto Clemente State Park	630
Sutton Place Synagogue	645
Columbia University Teachers College/ Horace Mann Auditorium	650
Diocese of the Armenian Church of America	660
Pace University	668
International House	670
Circle in the Square (Uptown)	680
New York School of Printing	700
Snug Harbor Cultural Center	700
New York City Mission Society, Mission Town House	716
American Academy and Institute of Arts and Letters	729
Columbia University/Ferris Booth Hall	748
City College of the City University of New York/ Aaron Davis Hall	750
The Concord Baptist Church (Brooklyn)	750
Norman Thomas High School (see Schools, Public)	750
Diplomat Hotel/Palm Room	800
Fashion Institute of Technology	800
High School of Art & Design	800
Jacob Riis Houses Amphitheater (plus standees)	800
New York State Theater (plus standees)	600/800
United Methodist Parish in Bushwick (Brooklyn)	800
New York Society for Ethical Culture	867
Queensborough Community College	871
The Community Church of New York	900
Diplomat Hotel/Grand Ballroom	900
92nd Street YM-YWHA	916
The College of Staten Island	918
Symphony Space, Inc.	922
Co-operative Auditorium	950
Roosevelt Auditorium	965
Martin Luther King Junior High School	984
Manhattan School of Music	988
Bronx High School of Science	1000
Congregational Church of North New York (Bronx)	1000
Eastern Christian Leasing Center	1000
Marymount College (Westchester)	1000
Alice Tully Hall/Lincoln Center for the Performing Arts	1096
Brooklyn Academy of Music/ Helen Carey Playhouse	1100
Entermedia Theater	1100
Hofstra University (Long Island)	1134
Truman High School (see Schools, Public)	1151
Stuyvesant High School (see Schools, Public)	1172
College of Mt. St. Vincent (Bronx)	1200
Columbia University/McMillan Theater	1200
Town Hall	1498
Hunts Point Palace (in each of 2 rooms)	1500
New York State Theater	1500
The Staten Island Ferry (seating capacity on boat)	1500
Julia Richman High School (see Schools, Public)	1502
Wagner College (Staten Island) (gymnasium)	1650
James Weldon Johnson Community Center, Inc. (outdoor Plaza theater)	2000
New York City Passenger Ship Terminal	2000
Terrace on the Park	2000
Brooklyn Academy of Music/Opera House	2100
Queens College/Colden Auditorium	2143
Hunter College Concert Bureau	692/2185
Lehman College Center for the Performing Arts (Bronx)	2310
Calderone Concert Hall (Long Island)	2400
Brooklyn College/Whitman Hall	2482
Washington Irving High School	2500
Beacon Theater	2618

Avery Fisher Hall/Lincoln Center for the Performing Arts	2738	Van Cortlandt Park Stadium	3600
City Center 55th Street Theater	2932	Iona College (Westchester)	4000
Fashion Industry High School	3000	Metropolitan Opera Association/Lincoln Center for the Performing Arts	4000
The Palladium	3387	Pratt Institute	5000
Roseland	3400	Radio City Music Hall	5882

Also see: AUDITORIUMS/CONFERENCE ROOMS/
        MEETING ROOMS (Seating 499 or less)
         HOTELS
         SCHOOLS
         STADIUMS

American Academy and Institute of Arts and Letters   368-5900
633 West 155th Street
New York, N.Y. 10032
Contact: Mrs. Edwina Williams, Office Manager

Auditorium
Seating capacity: 729
Rental fee: $250 for 3 hour performance May through September;
   $300 October through April. Rehearsal varies with time of day.
Stage, sound equipment, hardwood dance floor
Suggested uses: concert, lecture, recording session
Note: Tickets may be sold by subscription only. Parties are not allowed

Co-operative Auditorium   777-5530
551 Grand Street
New York, N.Y. 10002
Contact: Edward Ward

Auditorium, rehearsal space, ballroom
Seating capacity: 950; 30' x 20' of rehearsal space is available
Rental fee: $500 during day; $775 for Friday evening;
   $875 for Saturday evening
Stage, platform, piano, dance floor, kitchen; food may be served
Suggested uses: banquet, lecture, meeting, party, reception, wedding

District 1199   582-1890
Martin Luther King Jr. Labor Center   ext. 238
National Union of Hospital and Health Care Employees
310 West 43rd Street
New York, N.Y. 10011
Contact: Ms. Adele Kanter

Auditorium, meeting room, hall
Seating capacity: 500 for meeting/350 for dance in auditorium;
   150 for meeting in Walter Reuther Room; 450 for meeting/
   350 for dance in Eugene Debs Hall
Stage, ungraduated auditorium floor, piano, dance floor; catering
   is available
Suggested uses: meeting, performance, dance, etc.

Lehman College Center for the Performing Arts

Eastern Christian Leasing Center 665-1665
Savoy Manor 665-5666
120 East 149th Street
Bronx, N.Y. 10451
Contact: Jerome Green, Manager or Shirley Holmes, Assistant Manager

Auditorium, rehearsal space, conference room, meeting room,
 exhibit space, reception area
Seating capacity: 100/1000
Stage, platform, piano
Suggested uses: meeting, party, wedding, church service, gospel show

Educational Alliance, Inc. 475-6200
197 East Broadway ext. 220
New York, N.Y. 10002
Contact: Phyllis Drucker

Auditorium/gymnasium, rehearsal space, classrooms,
 conference room, roof garden, exhibit space
Seating capacity: 500 in auditorium; 200 on roof garden
Rental fee: $27.50 minimum on a weekday; varies with day,
 hours, and size of room
Stage, platform, piano, dance floor, motion picture projector, slide
 projectors, sound equipment, kitchen; food may be served
Suggested uses: all special events are possible

La Guardia Memorial House 534-7800
307 East 116th Street
New York, N.Y. 10029
Contact: Peter Pascale

Auditorium/gymnasium, classroom, lounge
Seating capacity: 500 in auditorium; 50 in classroom; 100 in lounge
Rental fee: maintenance charge
Stage, kitchen; food may be served
Suggested uses: concert, class, exhibit, lecture, meeting
Note: Space is only available to non-profit East Harlem community groups

Roosevelt Auditorium 477-3146
100 East 17th Street
New York, N.Y. 10003
Contact: Belle Horensen, President, Realty Corporation

Auditorium
Seating capacity: 950
Rental fee: varies
Platform
Note: Space is only available for meetings

* * * * * * *

BALLROOMS

New York Academy of Sciences	125	Sam & Esther Minskoff Cultural Center	400
Columbia University/Earl Hall Center	150	William Paterson College Student Center	400
Postgraduate Center West	175	Manhattanville College	500
Harkness House	200	Marc Ball Room	500
Jewish Center of Bayside Hills	200	Congregation B'nai Jeshurun	600
Temple Isaiah	200	Flushing Jewish Center	600
Workmen's Circle Building	200	Queens College Student Union	600
Manhattan Church of the Nazarene	220	The Ballroom at Windows on the World	1000
Seamen's Church Institute of New York	250	Oyster Bay & Crystal Palace	1000
Marymount Manhattan College	300	Terrace on the Park	2000
Sutton Place Synagogue	300	Hunts Point Palace	3000
District 1199	350	Sheraton Centre	3000
St. John's Hall	350	Roseland	3450

Also see: HOTELS

The Ballroom at Windows on the World   938-0032
One World Trade Center
106th floor
New York, New York 10048
Contact: Serge M. Baret, Director, Sales & Marketing

1,000 for receptions
600 for meetings
550 for a sit-down dinner
1,350 feet up into the air, 40,000 sq. ft. of space available for down to earth business meetings or floating parties.

Hunts Point Palace   328-3150
953 Southern Boulevard
Bronx, N.Y. 10459
Contact: Jocelin Flores, Manager

Ballroom
Seating capacity: 1000
Rental fee: varies
Stage, dance floor

Marc Ballroom   255-3400
27 Union Square
New York, N.Y. 10017
Contact: Morris Horn, Manager

Auditorium, ballroom
Seating capacity: 500
Rental fee: $900 for a weekend dance
Stage, piano, dance floor; food may be served
Suggested uses: all special events are possible except a class, fair, party, performance or promotion

Ballroom—Windows on the World

Oyster Bay & Crystal Palace 545-8402
31-01 Broadway 545-2990
Astoria, New York 11106
Contact: Banquet Manager

Main ballroom, meeting rooms
Seating capacity: 1500 theatre-style/1000 sitdown in main ballroom;
    50/1000 in meeting rooms
Food may be served only by caterer on premises
Suggested uses: meeting, dance, shower, christening, wedding

Roseland 247-0200
Roseland Amusement Company, Inc.
239 West 52nd Street
New York, N.Y. 10019
Contact: Anne Marie Cicciu, Director of Sales

Ballroom/arena, lounge, restaurant, parking lot
Seating capacity: 3,450 maximum capacity; 2,000 on dance floor
    plus 700 spectator seats; 1,600 cabaret style/2,000 theater style;
    250 standard exhibit booths can be accommodated on first floor
    (additional capacity on dance floor and Downstairs Lounge).
    196' x 95' arena area (including Terrace Restaurant); 112' x 55'
    dance floor; 15' ceiling to chandelier
15' x 23' roll-out stage, complete theatrical lighting and disco
    equipment, music and address systems, 2 movie and slide pro-
    jectors, 50' long bandstand, street level loading facilities,
    2 stand-up bars plus rolling bars; on premises kitchen food only
    may be served
Suggested uses: dance, exhibit, lecture, dinner, show

****

BOATS, BARGES & BALLOONS

The Ambrose Lightship 766-9020
South Street Seaport Museum
East River and Fulton Street
New York, New York 10038
Contact: David Beggs

One of the last active lightships in America
Guest capacity: 70
Bring own caterer

Peking

Bargemusic, Ltd. 737-7536
Fulton Ferry Landing
(Foot of Cadman Plaza West)
Brooklyn, New York

Barge
Seating capacity: 175 in 102' x 30' space
Rental fee: negotiable
Piano, large fireplace, wood panelled decor; food may be served
    by caterer of your choice
Suggested uses: meeting, conference, private party for corporate
    non-profit organizations as well as for individuals, film and
    photography shooting, fund-raising event
Main purpose of the barge is as a presentor of chamber music.
    Reconverted barge was formerly used to transport coffee
    for the Erie-Lackawanna Railroad and offers a panoramic view
    of the East River and Lower Manhattan

Bring Sailing Back, Inc. 825-1976
1 Broadway
New York, N.Y. 10004
Contact: Rosemarie Bechtold

"PETREL," a 70 ft. sailing yacht
Seating capacity: 34 during the day; 26 during the evening
Catered buffet and open bar
Suggested uses: class, meeting, party, reception, wedding, baptism,
    photographing advertisements on yawl, fund-raising, private charter,
    public sail

The Cabaret 246-4811
World Yacht Enterprises, Ltd.
14 West 55th Street
New York, New York 10019
Contact: J. Heap, President

A versatile, twin-decked 100' motor yacht suited to groups
    of 40 to 250.
Complete catering and bar service.
Additional boats available for entertaining from 2 to 2000 guests

Circle Line Sightseeing Yachts 563-3200
Pier 83
Foot of West 43rd Street
New York, N.Y. 10036
Contact: Rosalie Toguville

Seating capacity: 300/500
Rental fee: approximately $2,100 to $2,500; extra charge for catered party
Note: Boats are only available for three hour evening charter

Columbia 689-9292
Sparkman & Stephens
79 Madison Avenue
New York, N.Y. 10016
Contact: Judy Gallagher, Manager, Chartering Department

Classic vintage yacht suitable for formal affairs for up to 75 guests.
  Colorfully carpeted with 4 cabins, each has two single beds.
  Overnight accommodations for 9 persons. Charter will cost
  $2,000 minimum for 4 hours. Band and catering are available.
  Suitable for a weekend cruise

Haut Voyage Balloon (203) 673-1307
Pine Drive
Burlington, Connecticut 06013
Contact: Brian or Karin Boland

Wafting along the gentle air currents of the Hudson River Valley
  in a basket of a brilliantly-colored hot air balloon, with
  champagne landings at historic mansions, country inns and
  local vineyards. Hosted by a private "Chef de Picnique" and
  professional aeronauts who are pilots of the famed Champagne
  Tours of France.
Day and weekend excursions

Haut Voyage Balloons

Long Island Ferry Boat (516) 661-5061
at Captree Boat Basin (near Robert Moses
  beaches east of Jones Beach)
West Islip, N.Y. 11795
Contact: Caroline Bauer

"Captree Spray"
Seating capacity: 263
Rental fee: approximately $600 for first 100 persons, then
  per head charge for additional persons
Bar, enclosed lounge, dance floor, band facilities, sun deck
Boat can sail anywhere in the Great South Bay and up and down
  Fire Island for a four-hour charter from early Spring through
  the Fall. Daily excursions in summer. Fall schedule available.
Suggested uses: dinner/champagne cruise, fund-raiser, alumni
  reunion, sales meeting, company outing
Note: Mailing address is P.O. Box 204, West Islip, N.Y. 11795

The Mon Lei 840-7900
Chesapeke Bay and China Sea Towing Company
1040 Avenue of the Americas
New York, N.Y. 10036
Contact: Alen York

Chinese junk
Seating capacity: 100 on 60' vessel
Rental fee: $2,000 for 4 hours
Catering is available
Junk is 127 years old. Reminiscent of a Buddhist temple, the
 bulkheads and hull are decorated with authentic storytelling scrolls
Note: Only available for private parties dockside

Staten Island Ferry 248-8044
New York City Department of Marine and Aviation
Battery Maritime Building
New York, N.Y. 10004
Contact: Leonard Piekarsky, Commissioner

Staten Island Ferry
Seating capacity: 1500
Available for charter during July and August, occasionally
 September and October. Call for information.

Old Fashioned Mule Barges

Old Fashioned Mule Barges (215) 862-2842
New Hope Barge Co.
P.O. Box 164
New Hope, Bucks County, Pennsylvania 18938

The Delaware Canal, built in 1837, runs parallel to the Delaware River
 and is now a national historical landmark. In the 1860's some
 3000 boats and barges pulled by teams of mules were travelling
 the Canal.
Private parties aboard these barges emanate from New Hope, Pennsylvania.
Food may be served on the barge or at a secluded picnic area along
 the way. The barge is decorated with flowers and suitable
 live music may also be arranged.
Guest capacity: 80 maximum

Peking 766-9033
(sailing bark) 766-9020
Piers No. 15 and No. 16
East River
Contact: Judith Stonehill

Sailing vessel moored permanently
Seating capacity: 400/500 maximum can be accommodated on 377'
   long x 47' wide x 170'7" high from deck to mast vessel
Dance floor; food may be served by caterer of your choice. Vessel
   is restored, iron-hulled, four-masted and fully rigged
Suggested uses: all special events are possible except a professional dance

Pioneer

Pioneer 766-9078
(a 102' schooner)
16 Fulton Street
New York, N.Y. 10038
Contact: Joan Weller

Schooner
Seating capacity: 25
Food may be served
Built in 1885. View of N.Y. Harbor
Suggested uses: class, lecture, meeting, party, promotion,
   reception, wedding

The Purple Barge/Floating Foundation of Photography 737-7536
Pier 40 South (Hudson River) at West Houston and West Street
New York, N.Y.

A houseboat on top of a 36' x 159' steel barge.
   Multi-level decks, sundeck, walkways, gardens, stage;
   white nylon overhead for complete rain covering. Heated for
   winter functions.

Guest capacity: 400 maximum in summer; 75 maximum in winter
Food may be served by caterer of your choice
Suggested uses: all types of functions, cultural and social, including a wedding, performance, exhibit, dance, etc.

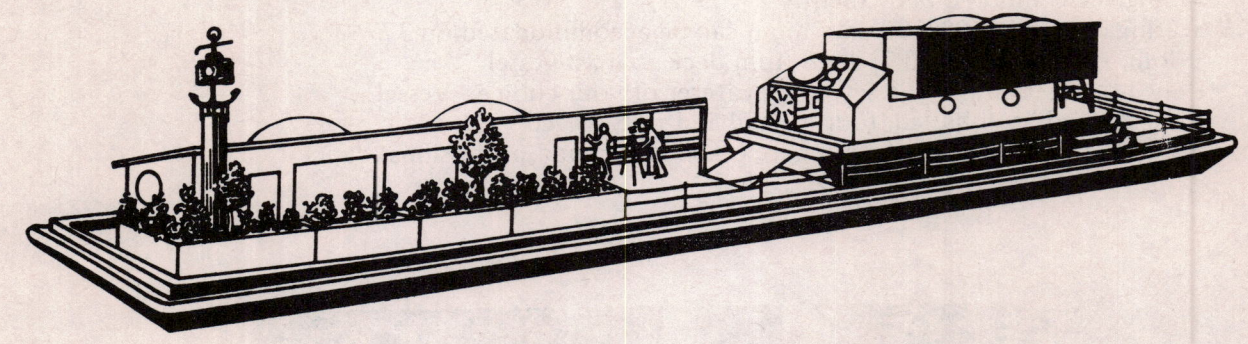

The Purple Barge

For additional information on boats see: PRIVATE PARTIES/PRIVATE PLACES and/or call (212) 737-7536

* * * * * * *

For CASTLES, MANSIONS AND HISTORIC HOUSES see:
    PRIVATE PARTIES/PRIVATE PLACES
    PRIVATE PARTIES/PUBLIC PLACES

For COUNTRY CLUBS & INNS see: PRIVATE PARTIES/PRIVATE PLACES

CHURCHES

MANHATTAN:

Cathedral Church of St. John the Divine   678-6996
Amsterdam Avenue & 112th Street
New York, N.Y. 10027
Contact: Ms. Lee Gorman, General Manager

Synod Hall, Undercroft, 3 meeting rooms, exhibit space,
    museum, cathedral, chapel, 13½ acres of grounds
Seating capacity: 800/1000 in Synod Hall; 300 auditorium-style
    in Undercroft; 40/80 in meeting rooms
Limited kitchen facilities; refreshments may be served by caterer
    on premises or bring your own
Suggested uses: concert, meeting, lecture
Note: Review by clergy may be necessary

St. John the Divine

Central Synagogue   838-5122
123 East 55th Street
New York, N.Y. 10022
Contact: Barry Kugel, Executive Director

2 auditoriums
Seating capacity: 380 in Vestry Auditorium; 450 in Beir Auditorium
Rental fee: reimbursement for out-of-pocket costs
Stage, piano, kitchen; food may be served
Suggested uses: concert, exhibit, lecture, meeting, performance, wedding
Note: Space is only available to philanthropic groups

Christ and St. Stephen's Church   787-2755
120 West 69th Street
New York, N.Y. 10023
Contact: Joan Lomaki

Auditorium
Seating capacity: approximately 250
Rental fee: varies
Raised stage, Steinway Grand Model M piano
Suggested uses: concert, wedding
Note: Space is only available on Thursday evenings and Sunday afternoons

Church Center for the United Nations 661-1762
777 United Nations Plaza (Room 10A)
New York, N.Y. 10017
Contact: Joan Fortenberry

Conference/meeting rooms, exhibit space, reception area, chapel
Seating capacity: 20/200 in conference rooms; 150 in chapel
Kitchen; food may be served
View of the U.N.
Suggested uses: all special events are possible including a wedding,
    memorial service, or seminar
Note: Space is only available to U.N.-related, non-profit, tax-exempt groups

Church of the Covenant 697-3185
310 East 42nd Street
New York, N.Y. 10017
Contact: Marion L. Maxfield

Parish hall, reception area, meeting rooms
Seating capacity: 150 in parish hall; 25/30 in meeting rooms
Stage, piano, kitchen; food may be served
Suggested uses: all special events are possible except a banquet,
    fair or promotion
Note: Space is only available to non-profit groups

The Church Within 580-3734
218 West 84th Street
New York, New York 10024
Contact: Rev. Larry King

2 rooms
Seating capacity: approximately 30 people may be accommodated
    in 17' x 21' space
Rental fee: $10 minimum per hour
Suggested uses: meditation, therapy, body work

The Community Church of New York 683-4988
40 East 35th Street
New York, N.Y. 10016
Contact: Mercedes Draisner

Auditorium, assembly hall, chapel
Seating capacity: 900 in auditorium; 180 in assembly hall; 60 in chapel
Stage, platform, piano
Suggested uses: concert, lecture, meeting, wedding

Congregation B'nai Jeshurun 787-7600
270 West 89th Street
New York, N.Y. 10024
Contact: Rhoda Beckman

Rehearsal space, ballroom, classroom, conference room, exhibit space,
  reception area, gymnasium
Seating capacity: 50/600
Rental fee: varies
Stages, platform, piano, dance floor, kitchen; kosher food only
  may be served
Suggested uses: all special events are possible

Diocese of the Armenian Church of America   **686-0710**
630 Second Avenue (at 34th Street)
New York, N.Y. 10016
Contact: Center Manager

Auditorium, rehearsal space, 5 classrooms, conference rooms,
  exhibit space, reception area
Seating capacity: 660 in auditorium; 200 maximum in classrooms
  and conference rooms
Stage, concert piano, dance floor, kitchen; food may be served
Suggested uses: banquet, conference, seminar, social dance, wedding

Good Neighbor Church   **369-0505**
119 East 106th Street
New York, N.Y. 10029
Contact: Rev. D. Rosado

Conference room
Seating capacity: 100/125
Rental fee: negotiable $100 donation to cover costs
Note: Space has limited availability. Political groups, smoking
  and alcoholic beverages are not allowed

Good Shepherd-Faith Presbyterian Church   **877-0685**
152 West 66th Street
New York, N.Y. 10023
Contact: Board of Deacons

Rehearsal space/social hall, conference room, sanctuary
Seating capacity: 100 in rehearsal space; 30/50 in conference room;
  300 in sanctuary
Rental fee: negotiable
Piano, dance floor, small kitchen; limited amount of food may be served
Suggested uses: concert, class, exhibit, lecture, meeting, performance,
  non-profit promotion, wedding coordinated with committee and pastor
Note: Rehearsal space has limited availability

Madison Avenue Baptist Church   **685-1377**
30 East 31st Street
New York, New York 10016
Contact: Pastor

Multi-purpose room
Seating capacity: 150
Proscenium stage, platform, piano
Suggested uses: auction, concert, class, exhibit, lecture, meeting,
  performance, rehearsal
Note: Space is only available to non-profit groups

Manhattan Church of the Nazarene 575-0300
(formerly the Lamb's Club)
130 West 44th Street
New York, N.Y. 10036
Contact: Caroline Ross, Executive Producer of Theater

Professional theater, ballroom, board room
Seating capacity: 350 in theater; 220 in ballroom; 20 in board room;
    125 in Sanctuary Restaurant
Stage, platform, piano, fireplace, kitchen; catering is available
    or bring your own
Suggested uses: banquet, theater performance, fund-raising
Note: Alcoholic beverages and smoking are not allowed

New York Society for Ethical Culture
2 West 64th Street
New York, N.Y. 10023
Contact: Jeanne Brown, Administrator

Auditorium, meeting room, library, social hall, ceremonial hall, balcony
Seating capacity: 867 in auditorium; 60 in 10' x 29' meeting room;
    60 in 6' x 28' library; 285 in social hall; 150 in 35' x 44'
    ceremonial hall
Rental fee: $500 to $600 for auditorium; $100 for meeting room;
    $100 for library; $400 to $450 for social hall; $250 for
    ceremonial hall
14' x 30' stage, platform, Steinway Grand Piano, PA system,
    dance floor, Wicks Pipe Organ, theatrical lighting, kitchen;
    food may be served
Suggested uses: memorial service, committee meeting, wedding, etc.
Note: Inquiries should be made in writing and should outline the
    general purposes of the group, its community service aspects and
    programs, tax status, and the date, time and number of persons
    anticipated

New York Society of the New Church (Swedenborgian) 685-8967
112 East 35th Street
New York, N.Y. 10016
Contact: Marion Priestnal

Small auditorium, rehearsal space, conference rooms, exhibit/recital hall
Seating capacity: 65 in auditorium
Rental fee: by contribution according to suggested scale
Stage, piano; food may be served on occasion
Small non-profit groups with compatible aims are encouraged
Note: Smoking is not allowed

Playhouse 46 246-7277
St. Clement's Theatre (at St. Clement's Church)
423 West 46th Street
New York, N.Y. 10036
Contact: Stephan Berwind

Theater
Seating capacity: 194
Stage, piano, dance floor, kitchen; food may be served
Suggested uses: auction, concert, class, lecture, meeting,
    performance, promotion, wedding

St. John's Hall 564-9070
210 West 31st Street
New York, N.Y. 10001
Contact: Don Brooks

Auditorium/ballroom/exhibit space, meeting rooms
Seating capacity: 350 in approximately 100 x 60 sq. ft. auditorium space;
    50/60 in meeting rooms
Proscenium stage, piano, dance floor, kitchen; food may be served
Suggested uses: all special events are possible including a flea market,
    except a performance, promotion or wedding

St. Mark's Church-in-the-Bowery 674-6377
Tenth Street & Second Avenue
New York, N.Y. 10003
Contact: Nora Lugo

Flexible theater space, open sanctuary, parish hall
Seating capacity: 60/80 in theater space; 500 in sanctuary;
    125 in parish hall; 40 x 80 sq. ft. of space is available
Rental fee: none except for a charge for a staff member to be present
Piano, hardwood dance floor, kitchen; food may be served
Note: Admission charges are not allowed

St. Peter's Church 935-2200
619 Lexington Avenue (at 54th Street)
New York, N.Y. 10022
Contact: Cathryn Mattson, Executive Director for theater or
    June Goldberg for all other spaces

Theater, music/rehearsal room, exhibit space, lounge/living room,
    sanctuary, terrace
Seating capacity: 199 in theater; 70 in music room; 150 in
    exhibit space; 150 in lounge; 300 in sanctuary
Rental fee: varies
Piano, dressing rooms, kitchen; food may be served
Suggested uses: concert, class, exhibit, lecture, meeting, party,
    performance, reception, wedding, film showing, staged reading

St. Philip's Community Service Council, Inc. 862-4943
207 West 133rd Street
New York, N.Y. 10030
Contact: Fr. Hinman

Church, auditorium, rehearsal space, conference room, exhibit space,
    lounge, asphalt parking lot
Seating capacity: 400 in auditorium; 20 in conference room
Rental fee: negotiable
16' x 36' outdoor stage, baby grand piano, sound equipment
Suggested uses: jazz concert, performance

St. Thomas Church 397-1660
1 West 53rd Street
New York, N.Y. 10019
Contact: Mrs. C. Schacht

Meeting room, church
Seating capacity: 100 in meeting room
Rental fee: varies
Small platform, piano; refreshments may be served
French Gothic style
Note: Space is not available for fund-raising or political events

St. Thomas

Salem Community Service Council, Inc. 678-2700
Salem United Methodist Church
2190 Seventh Avenue (at 129th Street)
New York, N.Y. 10027
Contact: Evelyn Brunson, Secretary of the Church

Auditorium, rehearsal space, sanctuary
Seating capacity: approximately 250 in auditorium
Rental fee: negotiable
Stage, platform, piano, motion picture projector, phonograph; food may be served

Sutton Place Synagogue 593-3300
225 East 51st Street
New York, N.Y. 10022
Contact: Mrs. H. Janover, Executive Director

Auditorium, rehearsal space, ballroom, exhibit space, reception area, board room
Seating capacity: 645 auditorium-style (may be divided); 300 in ballroom; 50 in board room
Platform, piano, dance floor, kitchen; kosher food only may be served
Suggested uses: all special events are possible

Universalist Church of New York 595-8410
4 West 76th Street
New York, N.Y. 10023
Contact: Dave Dunlop

Auditorium, theater, conference rooms, rehearsal space, gymnasium
Seating capacity: 500 in auditorium; 100 in theater; 12/75 in
   conference rooms; 150 in gymnasium
Rental fee: $300 for auditorium; $25 to $100 for conference room;
   $100 for gymnasium
Stage, platform, piano, sound equipment; food may be served

Washington Square Church 777-2528
133 West Fourth Street
New York, N.Y. 10012
Contact: Alex DiVincenti, Program Coordinator

Auditorium/sanctuary, meeting parlor
Seating capacity: 325 in auditorium; approximately 50 in meeting parlor
Piano, kitchen; food may be served
Suggested uses: concert, class, lecture, meeting, dance, performance,
   poetry reading

Also see: Columbia University, Millbank Chapel

BRONX:

Congregational Church of North New York 292-1950
411 East 143rd Street
Bronx, N.Y. 10454
Contact: Rev. Allison Phillips

Auditorium, rehearsal space, conference room, gymnasium
Seating capacity: approximately 1000 in auditorium; 300 in gymnasium
Rental fee: negotiable
Stage, piano, motion picture projector, film strip projector;
   food may be served

BROOKLYN:

The Cathedral of St. James 855-6390
Jay and Tillary Streets
Brooklyn, N.Y. 11201
Contact: Sr. Honora Nolty

2 meeting/seminar rooms, exhibit space
Seating capacity: 100 in Cathedral Center; 25 in smaller meeting room
Rental fee: varies
Suggested uses: concert, meeting, exhibit of works by painters,
   photographers and graphic artists

Church of St. Ann and The Holy Trinity 834-8794
122 Pierrepont Street (corner of Montague and Clinton Streets)
Brooklyn Heights, N.Y. 11201
Contact: Office, The Arts at St. Ann's

Parish hall, sanctuary
Seating capacity: 300 in Parish Hall; 1200 in sanctuary
Rental fee: varies with event
Stage, platform, piano, dance floor; food may be served
Space is an 1844 landmark
Suggested uses: all cultural and religious events are possible including an opera, ballet, dance or film showing except a promotion

The Concord Baptist Church   622-1818
833 Marcy Avenue
Brooklyn, N.Y. 11216
Contact: Wyatt Logan

Auditorium, rehearsal space, conference room, exhibit space, lounge
Seating capacity: 750
Rental fee: varies
Stage, platform, piano, motion picture projector, sound equipment, kitchen; food may be served

Congregation B'nai Sholom, Brooklyn   438-6922
Boro Park Progressive Synagogue
1515 - 46th Street
Brooklyn, N.Y. 11219
Contact: Rosalie Sabin

Conference room, exhibit space
Seating capacity: 100
Piano, dance floor, kitchen; kosher food only may be served
Suggested uses: auction, small banquet, concert, exhibit, lecture, meeting, party

Lutheran Church of the Risen Christ   498-3848
250 Blake Avenue
Brooklyn, N.Y. 11212
Contact: Rev. John Heinmeier

Auditorium, conference room/rehearsal space, playground, exhibit space
Seating capacity: 180 in auditorium; 30 in conference room; 100 in playground; 100 in exhibit space
Platform, piano
Suggested uses: concert, class, exhibit, lecture, meeting, performance, wedding

The Nazarene Congregational United Church of Christ   452-0306
MacDonough Street Community Center
506 MacDonough Street
Brooklyn, N.Y. 11233
Contact: Emily Brown

Hall, meeting rooms
Seating capacity: 240 in Fellowship Hall; approximately 75/115 in meeting rooms
Rental fee: $300 for fund-raising groups, $100 each additional hour/ $250 for 4 hours in hall for other groups, $75 each additional hour; $30 to $35 for meeting rooms for 2 hours, $5.00 each additional hour
Piano, kitchen; food may be served

People's Institutional A.M.E. Church   574-4200
236-244 Stuyvesant Avenue (at Madison Street)
Brooklyn, N.Y. 11221
Contact: Rev. Perkins

Auditorium, fellowship hall, rehearsal space, conference room,
    lounge/exhibit space
Seating capacity: 500 in auditorium; 150 in fellowship hall;
    12 in conference room
Stage, platform, piano, kitchen; food may be served
Suggested uses: all special events are possible except a party
Note: Alcohol is not allowed

St. John — St. Matthew Emanuel Community Center 768-0772
415 Seventh Street
Brooklyn, N.Y. 11215
Contact: David Smith, Coordinator

Auditorium, rehearsal space, sanctuary
Seating capacity: approximately 125 in auditorium; 250 in sanctuary
Rental fee: $10 per hour per room
Stage, platform, piano; food may be served
Suggested uses: concert, class, professional dance, exhibit, lecture,
    meeting, performance, reception, wedding

St. John's Episcopal Church 745-2377
9818 Fort Hamilton Parkway 745-5269
Brooklyn, N.Y. 11209
Contact: Rev. George Hoeh, Rector

Parish hall/auditorium/exhibit space, rehearsal space, conference room
Seating capacity: 150 in parish hall; 12 in conference room
Rental fee: by donation
Stage, piano, dance floor, kitchen; food may be served
Suggested uses: all special events are possible
Note: Space is only available during the evening

United Methodist Parish in Bushwick 574-6610
1139 Bushwick Avenue
Brooklyn, N.Y. 11221
Contact: Joyce Perry, Church Secretary or
    Garfield Huguley, Lay Leader

Sanctuary, rehearsal space
Seating capacity: 1500 in sanctuary
Rental fee: negotiable
Platform, pianos, sound equipment, pipe organ, kitchen;
    food may be served

QUEENS:

Temple Isaiah 544-2800
75-24 Grand Central Parkway
Forest Hills, N.Y. 11375
Contact: Marcia Weinroth, Administrator

Auditorium/meeting room, ballroom, rehearsal space, ballroom,
   classroom, conference room
Seating capacity: 75/100 in auditorium; 150/200 in ballroom;
   25 in classrooms and conference rooms
Rental fee: varies
Small stage, small platform, pianos, dance floor, kitchen;
   caterers available or bring your own
Suggested uses: all special events are possible

STATEN ISLAND:

All Saint's Church 698-1338
2329 Victory Boulevard
Staten Island, N.Y. 10314
Contact: Rev. Joel E.A. Novey

Auditorium/rehearsal space/conference room/exhibit space,
   grassy area, playground, reception area
Seating capacity: 50/100
Small dance floor, catered food may be served
Suggested uses: all special events are possible

Christ United Methodist Church 442-2033
1890 Forest Avenue 442-3755
Staten Island, N.Y. 10303
Contact: Church Office
      8 Eunice Place, Staten Island, N.Y. 10303

Auditorium, rehearsal space, conference room
Seating capacity: 300 in auditorium; 150 in conference room
Stage, piano, dance floor, kitchen; light refreshments may be served
Rental fee: minimum $75 donation plus minimal janitor fee for auditorium
Note: Space is only available to non-profit groups. Alcoholic beverages
   are not allowed

Prince of Peace Moravian Church 351-6500
Grimsby Street & Greeley Avenue
Staten Island, N.Y. 10306
Contact: Rev. Kenneth J. Hall, Pastor

Auditorium, hall
Seating capacity: 150 in auditorium; large open space in Main Hall
Rental fee: $50 maximum
PA system, kitchen

Reformed Church of Staten Island 442-7393
54 Richmond Avenue
Staten Island, N.Y. 10314
Contact: Pastor

Auditorium/sanctuary, meeting room, open space
Seating capacity: 500 in auditorium; 50/200 in meeting room
   and open space
Rental fee: by donation
Stage, motion picture projector, phonograph

St. John's Church Parish Hall 447-4430
1331 Bay Street
Staten Island, N.Y. 10305
Contact: Ethel Harker

Auditorium, conference room, grassy area, exhibit space
Seating capacity: 200 in auditorium; 10/40 in conference room
Stage, piano, dance floor, kitchen; food may be served
Suggested uses: class, exhibit, lecture, meeting, party,
    performance, reception

****

CONFERENCE CENTERS

Appel Farm Arts and Music Center (609) 358-2472
Elmer, N.J. 08318
Contact: Hannah Gross, Conference Chairperson

Conference center with overnight accommodations for 30 to 130 persons
Auditorium, 3 conference/classrooms, various outdoor areas, exhibit
    space, reception areas, dining hall, practice rooms, dormitories
Seating capacity: 250 in auditorium; 40 in each conference room;
    200 in dining area
Rental fee: $14 per person for groups over 150 in the spring and fall;
    $16 per person for groups of 25/150 for two or more days.
    Includes bedding supplies, 3 meals and a snack. $3.00 for linen
    and blanket; extra charge for use of auditorium
Stage, platform, piano, fireplace, dance floor, space's food only
    may be served in dining hall
All special events are possible including a sport event

Arden House

Arden House (212) 584-6464
Harriman Campus of Columbia University (914) 351-2171
Harriman, N.Y. 10926
Contact: Richard F. Kopacz, Manager

Complete conference center with overnight accommodations
    for 100 persons in the former estate of W. Averill Harriman
    and family
Note: Space is only available to non-profit groups

Bear Mountain Inn (914) 786-2731
Bear Mountain, N.Y. 10911
Contact: Conference Manager, Banquet Facilities

Complete conference center with overnight accommodations
    Sixty-five single rooms can accommodate 132 persons,
    double occupancy, daytime conference center can accommodate 500
    Various meeting rooms
    Rental fee: $83.50 per person single occupancy, includes 3 meals
        and meeting room; $72.50 per person double occupancy, includes
        3 meals and meeting room
    Space is owned and operated by the New York State Parks Commission

Carnegie Conference Center 572-8222
Carnegie Endowment for International Peace
30 Rockefeller Plaza, Room 5425
New York, N.Y. 10020
Contact: Kevin Cribley, Manager

Conference room
Seating capacity: 120, room may be partitioned
Rental fee: varies from $75 to $125 for 4 hours during the day;
    $125 to $250 for full day or evening
PA system, kitchen; food may be served by caterer of your choice
View of Central Park
Suggested uses: class, lecture, meeting, reception, executive luncheon
    or dinner
Note: Space is only available to non-profit, tax-exempt groups

College of Mount St. Vincent 549-8000
Riverdale, N.Y. 10471
Contact: Sister Margaret Angelovich

Auditorium
Seating capacity: 1200
Stage
Suggested uses: concert, meeting, lecture, wedding reception
Note: Space is occasionally available for summer conferences
    with an overnight capacity of 500

Deerpark Farms Resort (212) 586-2270
Galley Hill Road (914) 754-8357
Cuddebackville, N.Y. 12729
Contact: Romeo or Hanni Moncheur, Managing Owners

Resort can accommodate 250 during the day, 200 overnight
Auditorium, rehearsal space, ballroom, 10 classrooms,
    2 conference rooms, exhibit space, reception area, lounge,
    dining rooms, game rooms, tennis courts, heated swimming pool
Rental fee: upon request
Stage, piano, 2 fireplaces, 3 dance floors, kitchen; space's food only
    may be served
Suggested uses: all special events are possible including a seminar,
    workshop or family reunion

De Seversky Conference Center
Northern Boulevard
Old Westbury, New York 11568
Contact: Lawrence Q. Mahoney, Managing Director

(516) 626-1600

Conference center with overnight accommodations for 26 persons
   double occupancy
3 meeting rooms
Seating capacity: 75 in Ballroom; 20 in Library; 20 in Terrace Room
Platform, piano, fireplace, winding staircase, dance floor, kitchen;
   food may be served
Note: Space is only available for a class, lecture or meeting
   that has an educational purpose. Mailing address is
   P.O. Box 370, Old Westbury, N.Y. 11568

De Seversky Conference Center

Frost Valley YMCA
Oliverea, N.Y. 12462
Contact: Conference Registrar

(914) 985-7400

45 cabins, 10 lodges, conference hall, meeting rooms,
   2 dining halls, athletic grounds
4500 acres, including the "Castle," which has luxurious
   accommodations and the Gladys & Roger Straus Estate
   in adjoining valley which serves as additional conference site
Seating capacity: 300 in conference hall
Originally founded in 1901 as Camp Wawayanda for Boys,
   Frost Valley moved to its present location nearly three decades
   ago with the purchase of the Julius Forstmann Estate.
   Stone buildings have been renovated

A Graceful Inn/Conference Center
Millbrook, New York

(212) 737-7536

This Georgian estate on a hundred acre knoll with view
   of Dutchess County countryside is a country inn and
   conference center.
9 double rooms, 4 of which contain fireplaces, and 4 single
   rooms. All rooms furnished in period pieces.

A private paneled dining room furnished in the chippendale manner, winding staircase, quarry-tiled terrace.
The Conference Room is in a separate guest house isolated from the Inn. It is fully equipped for conference work.
Guest capacity: 22 for overnight; 70 for a conference/ approximately 100 for a social occasion
Pool and other recreational facilities.
This facility is especially popular for weddings.

A Graceful Inn/Conference Center

Harrison House Conference Center (516) 671-6400
Dosoris Lane
Glen Cove, New York 11542
Contact: Manager, Conference Center Services

Complete conference center can accommodate 200 persons. Space is a Long Island estate and manor house with overnight accommodations

The Henry Chauncey Conference Center (609) 921-3600
Educational Testing Service
Princeton, N.J. 08541
Contact: Conference Manager

Complete conference center with overnight accommodations for 200 persons, single or double occupancy. 400 acre campus consists of two separate structures for meetings: a modern two-story complex and a nineteenth-century barn that has been reconverted to an auditorium which seats 200 and can be subdivided. Cocktail lounge, dining room, game room, 2 tennis courts, outdoor swimming pool, sauna, gymnasium, terraces; audio-visual equipment is available. Especially suitable for educational purposes; banquets and private receptions can also be arranged
Note: Mailing address is P.O. Box 2605, Princeton, N.J. 08540

Holiday Hills (914) 855-1550
Pawling, N.Y. 12564
Contact: Conference Manager

Conference and vacation center with overnight accommodations for 200 persons. Two dining rooms accommodate from 50 to 200 persons. Auditoriums, meeting rooms, library, lounge areas. 12 tennis courts are situated on 550 acres which are suitable for a conference, training event, seminar, reunion or retreat. Extensive outdoor recreational facilities. Overlooks Berkshire foothills and Green Mountain Lake. Rates are reasonable at this center which is a branch of the YMCA of Greater New York

Hominy Hill Golf Course (201) 842-4000
Monmouth County Park System
P.O. Box 326
Newman Springs Road
Lincroft, N.J. 07738
Contact: Robert Decker or Tom Higgins

Daytime conference center comprising two floors
Classrooms, conference room, meeting room, patio, golf course, reception area, library, living room, dining room
Seating capacity: 30 in meeting rooms; 125 in dining room
Rental fee: $75 during the day; $85 during the evening for use of the conference center; dining room included in meal charge
Dance floor, kitchen; food may be served
Suggested uses: all special events are possible including a reception, business lunch or wedding, except an auction, concert, fair, or performance

International Center 986-8371
345 East 46th Street
New York, N.Y. 10017
Contact: Christine Velasquez or Michele Greene

Auditorium, conference room, exhibit space, roof terrace, lounge
Seating capacity: 20/400
Rental fee: varies with time
Platform, PA system, kitchen; food may be served
Suggested uses: dinner, luncheon, class, exhibit, promotion, reception, meeting, workshop
Note: Space is only available to non-profit, tax-exempt groups

International House 678-5077
500 Riverside Drive
New York, N.Y. 10027
Contact: Sukie Rubio

Daytime conference center (Home Room, Mural Room, West Room)
Auditorium, meeting rooms, recital room, auditorium foyer
Seating capacity: 350 for meals/670 sitdown in auditorium (flexible seating); 75/80 in meeting rooms; 125 in auditorium foyer
Rental fee: varies with function, time and nature of group
Stage, platform, piano, dance floor
Small kitchen, cafeteria; private dining
Suggested uses: dance, meeting, reception, performance, recital, wedding

Mohonk Mountain House (914) 255-1000
Mohonk Lake (212) 233-2244
New Paltz, N.Y. 12561
Contact: Libby Long, Sales Director

Complete conference center with overnight accommodations for 500
   persons. Various sized meeting rooms, conference rooms, exhibit
   space and reception area. Many of the rooms have fireplaces.
   A piano and dance floor are also on the premises. Private dining
   is available. Rental rates upon request. View of valley lake and the
   Catskill Mountains. Facility was established in 1869 and is ninety
   miles from New York City

Seven Springs Center (914) 241-1880
Oregon Road
Mt. Kisco, N.Y. 10549
Contact: Joan Chandler

Complete conference center with overnight accommodations for
   35 persons. This facility consists of 2 stone mansions on the
   former estates of Eugene and Agnes Meyer and of Henry J. Heinz, II.
   It is open to groups which are non-profit with educational and
   cultural purposes in return for a contribution determined with the
   center in each case. The center does not have a fee schedule

Sterling Forest Conference Center (914) 351-4777
R.R. No. 1
Sterling Lake Road
Tuxedo, N.Y. 10987
Contact: Eleanor Lynch

Complete conference center with overnight accommodations
Auditorium, classroom, conference room, tennis courts, exhibit
   space, reception area, gymnasium, game room, terrace
Fifty-five rooms can accommodate 100 persons
Overnight rates are $90 twin/$135 single on a Full American Plan
Platform, dance floor, fireplace, kitchen; food may be served
All special events are possible except an auction, professional dance
   or fair
View of lake. Facility is 30 miles from New York City

Tarrytown House

Tarrytown House (914) 591-8200
Executive Conference Center
East Sunnyside Lane
Tarrytown, N.Y. 10591
Contact: Director of Sales

Complete conference center with overnight accommodations
One-hundred-and-thirty-five rooms can accommodate 270 persons
 double occupancy
Twenty-five conference rooms accommodate 5 to 200 persons;
 recreational facilities are on the premises
Overnight rates are $105 per person double occupancy; $135 per person
 single occupancy; $40 per person for day meeting
Complete audio-visual equipment
26 acre estate which was built in 1840 and was the home of Mary Duke Biddle
 overlooks the Hudson River and is 20 miles north of New York City

Also see: The Faculty House
> **HOTELS**
> **SCHOOLS AND COLLEGES**
>
> For national listings call: (212) 737-7536

* * * * * * *

DISCOS/SUPPER CLUBS

Bentley's   684-2540
25 East 40th Street
New York, N.Y. 10016
Contact: Dolores Juliano, Proprietress

Reception area, workshop/dinner room
Seating capacity: 140/250 formal seating on 2 levels
Rental fee: varies with function
Stage, platform, dance floor, kitchen; food may be served
Suggested uses: banquet, social dance, lecture, meeting, party,
 reception, wedding, corporate function

Brandi   564-0408
1055 Washington Avenue
Brooklyn, N.Y.
Contact: Anthony Cooper, President

Rehearsal space, ballroom, party room, bar
Seating capacity: 250
Rental fee: negotiable; $350 minimum depending on day and function
Stage, platform, dance floor; food may be served
Suggested uses: concert, social or professional dance, exhibit,
 party, reception, wedding

Copacabana   755-6010
10 East 60th Street
New York, N.Y. 10022
Contact: Peter Dorn, Vice President

Rehearsal space, ballroom, conference room, reception area,
    workshop/banquet space
Seating capacity: 1000 cocktail seating on 2 levels; 380 lower level/
    150 upper level formal seating
Stage, platform, piano, winding staircase, dance floor, kitchen;
    food may be served
Parking across the street
Suggested uses: all special events are possible including corporate parties

Electric Circus Disco/Club   989-9505
100 Fifth Avenue (at 15th Street)
New York, N.Y. 10011
Contact: Deborah Day

Theater in the round, rehearsal space, ballroom, exhibit space,
    reception area, restaurant
Seating capacity: 250 sitdown dinner/1500 disco party
Rental fee: negotiable
Stage, platform, winding staircase, dance floor; food may be served,
    catering is available
Suggested uses: all special events are possible

Interferon Nightclub   620-0515
30 West 21st Street
New York, New York 10010
Contact: Ron Martinez, Director

Auditorium, ballroom, exhibit space, reception area, restaurant
Seating capacity: 220 on each of 3 floors
Rental fee: negotiable according to event
Stage, platform, dance floor, state of the art sound and video
    systems, kitchen; food may be served
Note: All special events are possible including a fashion show
    and three camera video productions

Justine   695-9229
500 Eighth Avenue (at 36th Street)
New York, N.Y. 10001
Contact: Harold Dow, Manager, Norman Dow, Manager or
    Dawne Steward, Administrative Assistant

Rehearsal space, ballroom
Seating capacity: 200
Rental fee: negotiable; 450 minimum depending on day and function
Platform, dance floor; food may be served by caterer of your choice
Suggested uses: social or professional dance, exhibit, party,
    performance, reception, wedding

Large Art Deco Nightclub/Entertainment Complex   737-7536
New York, New York

Located on the 4th floor of a solid industrial building
    in the Chelsea area, this highly sophisticated facility
    offers 3 cocktail lounges, dining rooms and disco.
    Abundant fresh floral arrangements are part of the
    high-style decor. Private dining areas may be arranged
    with guests later joining open disco area.

Large Art Deco Nightclub/Entertainment Complex

Guest capacity: 20/2000
All manner of functions are appropriate including a theme
   party, bar mitzvah, corporate party, fashion show, benefit
   or a wedding
Note: Space is only available Wednesdays through Sundays

Leviticus International Entertainment Complex 564-0408
45 West 33rd Street
New York, N.Y. 10001
Contact: C. Mal Woolfolk, Owner or Bob Cherry, Manager

Rehearsal space, reception area, disco/cabaret
Seating capacity: 175; space can hold 446
Rental fee: negotiable; $500 maximum Monday through Friday;
   $800 on Sunday
Platform, piano, dance floor; food may be served
Suggested uses: auction, social or professional dance, exhibit,
   meeting, party, performance, promotion, reception,
   wedding, film and advertisement background

Multi-Media Party Space in the West 80's 737-7536
New York, N.Y.

Seating capacity: 400
Rental fee: negotiable
Stage, platform, piano, dance floor, game room, complete
   sound equipment to handle live music presentations, light show,
   dual image slide projection show, 2 bars; food may be served
   by caterer of your choice
Suggested uses: all special events are possible including a live
   music showcase, except a banquet or fair

New York, New York Disco and Restaurant 245-2400
29-33 West 52nd Street (disco)
New York, N.Y. 10019 247-2550
Contact: Michael Kirvan, Owner (restaurant)

Rehearsal space, conference room, exhibit space, restaurant
Seating capacity: 250/700 in disco; 125/400 in restaurant
Rental fee: varies
Stage, platform, piano, dance floor, kitchen; food may be served
Suggested uses: all special events are possible except an auction,
   class, professional dance or fair

Pippin's 753-8898
5 East 54th Street
New York, N.Y. 10022
Contact: Andy Hollick, Owner

Reception area
Seating capacity: varies
Dance floor, kitchen; food may be served
Suggested uses: banquet, social dance, party, promotion,
   reception, wedding, corporate cocktail/meal

Reflections 688-3365
40 East 58th Street
New York, N.Y. 10022
Contact: Arthur Meola, Manager

Disco, reception area
Seating capacity: 105 formal seating
Rental fee: varies with event
Dance floor, kitchen; food may be served
Suggested uses: banquet, social or professional dance, party,
   reception, wedding, holiday and corporate functions

Regine's   826-0990
502 Park Avenue (at 59th Street)   688-0516
New York, N.Y. 10022   (banquet office)
Contact: Philip Gaziano, Banquet Manager

Ballroom (Crystal Room)
Seating capacity: 100/220
Rental fee: negotiable
Stage, dance floor, kitchen; food may be served
   only by space's own caterer
Suggested uses: all special events are possible including
   fashion shows except a concert, class, fair or lecture

Xenon   221-2690
124 West 43rd Street
New York, N.Y. 10036
Contact: Jeff Kiehl, Office Manager

Disco room
Seating capacity: approximately 1,500
Dance floor
Suggested uses: auction, banquet, concert, social dance, party,
   performance, reception, wedding
Note: Admission fees are only allowed by charities

* * * * * * *

ENVIRONMENTAL CENTERS

Asphalt Green Youth, Sports and Arts Center   369-1617
90th Street and York Avenue   348-1990
New York, N.Y. 10028   (Centrone)
Contact: Phil Centrone or Jerry Siegel   876-9440
    (Siegel)
Regulation-size football field
Rental fee: $20 per hour
Space is a community sponsored recreation center
Suggested uses: soccer, volleyball, basketball, etc.

Caumsett Mansion   (212) 520-7240
Queens College Center for Environmental Teaching and Research   (516) 421-3526
Caumsett State Park
Huntington, N.Y. 11743
Contact: Dr. Philip White, Director

Georgian style mansion built in 1925. Former home of Marshall Field III.
   Surrounded by 1600 acres of forests, meadows, pond and beach.
Facility can accommodate 35 persons overnight, approximately 100
   for a meeting during the day
Note: Space is only available for an environmentally related
   conference or workshop

Landscaped Terraces & View of Hudson River at Wave Hill Environmental Center

Fireboathouse Environmental Center   876-9440
(footed at 90th Street on the East River)
New York, N.Y. 10028
Contact: David Mosher, Director

This facility is part of the Asphalt Green Youth, Sports and Arts Center
Note: Facility has limited availability

Gateway National Recreation Area
Floyd Bennet Field
Brooklyn, N.Y. 11234
Headquarters

Any group seeking to utilize facilities for special activities belonging to the Gateway National Recreation Area must make application for a permit by contacting the Area Manager of each unit. Events seeking permit should be educational, recreational or cultural in nature and must be free of charge. Group must be non-profit and tax-exempt. Tours and various other group events are also regularly held by the individual units

Jamaica Bay Unit   630-0126
Contact: Area Manager

Canarsie Pier — available for cultural events which are free of charge to the public. Stage and sound system may be made available

Floyd Bennet Field — its several aircraft hangars may be made available for sport or exhibit functions, public gatherings

Sandy Hook Unit   (201) 872-0115
Contact: Area Manager

Fort Hancock — historic fort on picturesque site offers magnificent view of Manhattan. Oldest operating lighthouse nearby

Fort Hancock Post Theater — theatrical performances

Staten Island Unit   351-8700
Contact: Area Manager

Conference rooms, beach area, grassy area, ball fields, tennis courts, parking lot
Seating capacity: 20/70 in conference rooms

Wave Hill Center for Environmental Studies   737-7536
675 West 252nd Street
Bronx, New York 10471
Contact: Florence Smeraldi, Manager of Operations

Built in the early 19th century as a family estate for William Lewis Morris and lived in by publisher William Appleton, writer Mark Twain and others, Wave Hill was a gathering place for thinkers and notables. Overlooking the Hudson and the Palisades, this 150-year-old New York City property was later founded as an arboretum and botanic garden. Its mansion is a two-story fieldstone house designed in the Greek Revival style, with Armor Hall providing an excellent setting for indoor functions.
Auditorium/ballroom/concert hall, 3 conference rooms, patio, garden, exhibit space, reception areas, dining room
Platform, piano, dance floor, kitchen; food may be served by caterer of your choice
Suggested uses: outdoor and indoor motion picture shooting and fashion photography, guided tours

Note: Space is available to non-profit groups and corporate members for a meeting, conference, lecture, etc., on weekdays; weekends after 4:30 p.m. For special functions, the facility is available on a one-time per year basis to corporate and profit making groups upon payment of a corporate membership contribution. Individual private events such as weddings are not allowed

* * * * * * *

EXHIBITIONS/EXPOSITIONS

Abraham Goodman House
Actor's Playhouse
Adelphi Academy (Brooklyn)
All Saint's Church (Staten Island)
American Place Theater
American Standard Exhibition Center
Appel Farm Arts & Music Center (New Jersey)
Armories
Artists Space
Association of Artist-Run Galleries, Inc.
The Barbizon
Barbizon Plaza Hotel
Bard College (Westchester)
Bard Hall
Beacon Theatre
Bloomingdale House of Music
Bronx Museum of the Arts
Brooklyn Museum/Community Gallery
Brooklyn YMCA
The Buckley School
C.W. Post Center of Long Island University (Long Island)
Calderone Concert Hall (Long Island)
Cami Hall
The Cathedral of St. James (Brooklyn)
Cathedral Church of St. John the Divine
Central Queens YMCA
Central Synagogue
Church Center for the United Nations
Church of the Covenant
City Center 55th Street Theater
Colonnades Theatre Lab, Inc.
Concord Baptist Church (Brooklyn)
Congregation B'nai Jeshurun
Congregation B'nai Shalom (Brooklyn)

Congregational Church of North New York (Bronx)
Cultural Affairs Department
Dennis Wayne Dancer's School
Diocese of the Armenian Church of America
Diplomat Hotel
District 1199
Donnell Library Center
Dramatis Personae
Drew Hamilton C.Y.O. Community Center
East Flatbush Rugby Y (Brooklyn)
East River Savings Bank
East/West Center
Eastern Christian Leasing Center
Educational Alliance, Inc.
Electric Circus Disco/Club
Entermedia Theater
Equitable Gallery
Ethical Humanist Society of Long Island
Exhibition/Hospitality Railroad Car
Fashion Institute of Technology
Fifth Avenue Hotel
Flushing Jewish Center (Queens)
Fraunces Tavern Museum
Gateway National Recreation Area/ Floyd Bennet Field (Brooklyn)
Gimbel's East
Hotel Overlooking Gramercy Park
Greenwich House Music School
Grolier Club
Gulbenkian Cultural Center
Gustave Hartman YM-YWHA (Queens)
Hammarskjold Plaza
Harlem State Office Building
Hudson Guild

New York Exposition & Convention Center

Institute for Art and Urban Resources, Inc./
    Project Studios One (P.S. 1)
International House
Iona College
Jamaica Arts Center (Queens)
James Weldon Johnson Community Center
Jewish Center of Bayside Hills (Queens)
The Jewish Museum
LaGuardia Community College (Queens)
La Guardia Memorial House
Langston Hughes Community Library and
    Cultural Center
Lehman College Center for the Performing Arts
Library and Museum of the Performing Arts
Light Opera of Manhattan
Long Island University – Brooklyn
Lutheran Church of the Risen Christ
    (Brooklyn)
Madison Avenue Baptist Church
Madison Square Garden
Manhattan Punch Line
Marymount College
Metropolis Roller Skate Club
Metropolitan Republican Club
Sam & Esther Minskoff Cultural Center
Morse Mime Theater
Mosholu-Montefiore Community Center (Bronx)
Museum of Holography
Nassau Veterans Memorial Coliseum
    (Long Island)
New York Academy of Sciences
New York City Passenger Ship Terminal
New York Coliseum
New York Exposition & Convention Center
New York Public Transit Exhibit
    (Brooklyn)
New York Society of the New Church
New York University/Loeb Student Center
112 Workshop, Inc.
The Oval Room
The Palladium
Park Circle Roller Skating Rink (Brooklyn)
Parson's School of Design (Midtown Campus)
Path/World Trade Center Terminal
People's Institutional A.M.E. Church
    (Brooklyn)

Pioneer
Pratt Institute
Recently Restored Landmark Hotel
Queens College Student Union
The Queens Museum
Queensborough Community College
Radio City Music Hall
Restored Village (Staten Island)
Richard Allen Center for Culture & Art
Riverdale-Yonkers Society for Ethical
    Culture (Bronx)
Roberto Clemente State Park (Bronx)
Roseland
St. Hilda's & St. Hugh's School
St. John's Church Parish Hall (Staten Island)
St. John's Episcopal Church (Brooklyn)
St. John's Hall
St. John's University (Staten Island)
St. Mary's Manhattanville Episcopal Church (Bronx)
St. Peter's Church
St. Peter's Episcopal Church
St. Phillip's Community Service Council,
    Inc.
Seamen's Church Institute of New York
Sloane House YMCA
Snug Harbor Cultural Center (Staten Island)
Studios 58 Playhouse, Inc.
Subway Mezzanines as Exhibit Places
Terrace on the Park
13th Street Theatre
Union Square Theatre
United Nations Plaza Hotel
Vandam Theater, SoHo
Wagner College (Staten Island)
Wave Hill Center for Environmental
    Studies (Bronx)
White Mask Theatre Corporation
Willkie Memorial Building
Workmen's Circle Building
World Trade Center
YM & YWHA of Williamsburg, Inc.
    (Brooklyn)
Young Men's Christian Association,
    McBurney Branch

American Standard Exhibition Center   840-5201
40 West 40th Street
New York, N.Y. 10018
Contact: Cyndy Cesena, Public/Investor Relations Coordinator

Exhibit space
Rental fee: none

Artists Space 226-3970
105 Hudson Street
New York, N.Y. 10013
Contact: Susan Wyatt, Associate Director

Exhibit space, reception area
Seating capacity: 150
Rental fee: negotiable
Suggested uses: all special events are possible including a film screening,
 except a banquet, fair, promotion or wedding

The Bronx Museum of the Arts 364-7700
851 Grand Concourse
Bronx, N.Y. 10451
Contact: Carmen Vega Torres

Rotunda/exhibit space, reception area
Seating capacity: 100
Piano; food may be served
Space is a landmark rotunda
Suggested uses: concert, class, exhibit, lecture, theatre or dance
 performance, reception, workshop
Note: Museum is in the rotunda of the Bronx courthouse. Fund-
 raising events are not allowed

Brooklyn Museum 638-5000
Community Gallery ext. 229
200 Eastern Parkway
Brooklyn, N.Y. 11238
Contact: Richard Waller, Coordinator

Exhibit space in the Community Gallery
Rental fee: none
Note: Space is only available for group exhibitions primarily
 by Brooklyn artists

East River Savings Bank 553-9768
26 Cortlandt Street
New York, N.Y. 10007
Contact: Mrs. Guilfoyre

Exhibit space, reception area

>World Trade Center 553-9848
>Concourse
>New York, N.Y. 10048
>Contact: James Buechler
>
>Exhibit space
>
>110 William Street 553-9802
>New York, N.Y. 10038
>Contact: Ms. Quiñones
>
>Exhibit space, reception area
>
>60 Spring Street 553-9801
>New York, N.Y. 10038
>Contact: Nickie Fung
>
>Exhibit space, reception area

　　　　41 Rockefeller Plaza　　　　　　　　　　　　　　　　　　553-9817
　　　　New York, N.Y. 10020
　　　　Contact: Mr. Lapinski
　　　　Exhibit space

　　　　743 Amsterdam Avenue　　　　　　　　　　　　　　　　553-9838
　　　　New York, N.Y. 10025
　　　　Contact: Nelson Badillo
　　　　Exhibit space

Note: All of these spaces are only available for non-profit,
　non-commercial purposes

Equitable Gallery　　　　　　　　　　　　　　　　　　　　　554-4416
1285 Avenue of the Americas (at 51st Street)　　　　　　　　　　(Mackri)
New York, New York 10019　　　　　　　　　　　　　　　　　 554-3520
Contact: Frank Mackri, Director of Graphic Arts or Ellen Hsiao　　(Hsiao)

Lobby exhibit space
Request for use must be made in writing at least one year
　in advance
Note: Space is only available on weekdays. Non-profit groups
　are particularly welcome

Exhibition/Hospitality Railroad Car　　　　　　　　　　　　(212) 737-7536

For display of equipment and manufactured goods.
　This car moves on regular Amtrak passenger tracks
　into the center of major cities; i.e., near the Chicago Loop,
　New Orleans Superdome or Madison Square Garden
　in Manhattan
The Virginia Beach, a sleeping-dining-lounge car, is also available
　for corporate or public travel

Grolier Club　　　　　　　　　　　　　　　　　　　　　　　　838-6690
47 East 60th Street
New York, N.Y. 10022
Contact: Librarian

Exhibition hall
Seating capacity: 100
Rental fee: upon request
Note: Space is only available to book-oriented groups

New York Coliseum　　　　　　　　　　　　　　　　　　　　757-5000
Columbus Circle
New York, N.Y. 10019
Contact: James Torres, Managing Director of the Coliseum
　Exhibition Corporation

Exhibit halls, meeting rooms
Seating capacity: varies
Rental fee: varies
Suggested uses: lecture, conference, trade fair, public show

New York Exposition and Convention Center   930-0303
Between 11th and 12th Avenues and 34th-39th Streets
New York, N.Y. 10001
Contact: Convention Center Development Corporation,
   Public Relations Department

Exhibition space
Seating capacity: 140,000 sq. ft. of space available for 35,000
   people in meeting and special events rooms; total floor area is
   1.8 million sq. ft. (500,000 sq. ft. on Upper Level, 250,000 sq. ft.
   on Lower Level); 1 acre outdoor plaza, on-site kitchens
This will be the largest exhibition space ever contained within
   a single building. Panoramic view of waterfront.
Note: The architects are I.M. Pei & Partners Lewis, Turner
   Partnership. Opening date of this $375,000,000 center is Spring 1984.

Path (Port Authority Trans-Hudson Corp.)   466-7652
World Trade Center Terminal
One World Trade Center
New York, N.Y. 10048
Contact: Myron L. Hurwitz, Supervisor of Passenger Services
   and Community Programs

Public space
60' x 60' space is available in PATH rail transit terminal
   at World Trade Center
Suggested uses: exhibit, free performances during evening
   rush hour for riders

Pratt Institute   636-3771
Brooklyn, N.Y. 11205   636-3772
Contact: Ron Jabusch for rehearsal space, gymnasium/open space,   (Jabusch)
   classrooms, dance studios, Activity Center, athletic field;
   Stratton Lee, Vice President, Campus Management, for   636-3777
   auditorium and lounge; or Ellen Schwartz for exhibit space   (Lee)

    636-3517
Auditorium, rehearsal space, 2 exhibit spaces, gymnasium/open   (Schwartz)
   space, classrooms, lounge, 2 dance studios, Activity Center,
   athletic field
Seating capacity: 500 in auditorium; 50/150 in exhibit spaces;
   200 in lounge; 5,000 in Activity Center
Rental fee: varies
PA system
Suggested uses: exhibit, meeting, conference, athletic event,
   demonstration

St. John's University, Staten Island Campus   447-4343
300 Howard Avenue
Staten Island, N.Y. 10301
Contact: William Stone, Librarian

Exhibit space in Loretto Memorial Library
Rental fee: none; liability insurance must be provided

White Columns   924-4212
325 Spring Street
New York, N.Y. 10012
Contact: Joshua Baer

Exhibit space
Seating capacity: approximately 125
Food may be served
Suggested uses: all special events are possible including an artist
    workshop, except an auction, banquet or wedding. Dance is discouraged

The World Trade Center   466-4233
The Port Authority of New York and New Jersey
1 World Trade Center
New York, N.Y. 10048
Contact: Marie Putigrano, Public Services Coordinator

2 lobbies, outdoor plaza
Seating capacity: 20,000 sq. ft. and 8,000 sq. ft. of space
    is available in lobby of The World Trade Center; 5 acres
    of space is available in outdoor plaza
Rental fee: upon request
Stage, platform, piano, sound equipment may be available, display system
Suggested indoor uses: art and small product-type exhibition; small trade show
Suggested outdoor uses: fair, performance, sizeable equipment display

Also see: ARMORIES
            HOTELS

****

CLOCK TOWERS

The Institute for Art and Urban Resources, Inc.

The Institute for Art and Urban Resources, Inc.   233-1096 (clocktower)
The Clocktower   784-2084 (office)
108 Leonard Street
New York, N.Y. 10013
Contact: Allana Heiss, President and Executive Director
    or Ron Lynch

Unique exhibition space for one-man shows in what used to be
the old New York Federal Building. Lower gallery's walls
are 13 ft. high; clocktower's walls are 25 ft. high.
Total footage is under 3000 ft.
Artists are encouraged to submit documentation and proposals
for the showing of their work in writing to the offices at
P.S. 1, 46-01 21st Street, Long Island City, N.Y. 11101.
Space is open Wednesday through Saturday, 1:00 p.m. to 6:00 p.m.

* * *

EXHIBITS: OUTDOORS

Some of the major outdoor art exhibits in New York City are:

Art Carnival at Lincoln Center — 765-5100
Leonard DePaur
1865 Broadway, 11th floor
New York, N.Y. 10023

Brooklyn Botanic Garden Fence Art Show — 622-4433
1000 Washington Avenue
Brooklyn, N.Y. 11225

Central Park Outdoor Art Exhibit — 675-2318
Bill Silver
278 West 19th Street
New York, N.Y. 10011

Gracie Square Art Exhibit — contact in writing
Laura C. Mayer
500 East 87th Street
New York, N.Y. 10028

Lincoln Center Plaza Arts and Crafts Exhibit — (212) 765-5100
American Concern for Artistry & Craftsmanship
P.O. Box 20
Hasbrouck Heights, N.J. 07604

Promenade and Fine Arts Exhibition — 783-4469 / 783-3077
Brooklyn Arts and Culture Association
The Brooklyn Museum
200 Eastern Parkway
Brooklyn, N.Y. 11238

Washington Square Outdoor Art Show — 982-6255
33 Fifth Avenue
New York, N.Y. 10003

* * *

FAIRGROUNDS, FLEA MARKETS & STREET FAIRS

FAIRGROUNDS

Dutchess County Fair Grounds (914) 876-4001
Route 9
Rhinebeck, New York 12572
Contact: Mr. Odak, Manager

140,000 acres of fair grounds, bandstand, stage, enclosed
  buildings, etc. Available May through October
Guest capacity: 50,000

FLEA MARKETS

For Flea Market location information in New York City
  write to:

> Department of Consumer Affairs
> 80 Lafayette Street
> New York, New York 10013
> Attn: Grace Davis, Computer Association

STREET FAIRS

Street Activity Permit 566-2506
Community Liaison Unit 566-2507
51 Chamber Street, Room 608
New York, N.Y. 10007
Contact: Apply at your local Community Board office. To find
  out where your Board office is located, or for general information,
  call or write the Community Liaison Unit above

Any community groups or block association may apply for a Street Activity Permit to close a street for a special event. Applicant must be over 21 years of age, a duly authorized group representative, and apply in person at least four to six weeks prior to the scheduled event at their local Community Board. If a community group or block association is not the applicant, a majority of the residents and/or merchants on the block must approve the proposed street closing. Processing fee is $10.00

Basic requirements for a street closing:

Street should *not* have a bus route, fire lane, garage or parking lot in use during closing hours. It should preferably not have active driveways, high volume of traffic or two-way traffic nor should it be near another closed street

Other permits and/or approvals which may be required:

Barricades and No Parking Signs — Local police precinct will give information for posting No Parking signs. It is illegal to restrict access to the street by obstructions such as garbage cans or automobiles. Emergency vehicles must have access if needed

Beer Permit — Sponsoring group needs to obtain a license for selling beer from:

The New York City Alcoholic Beverage Control Board 2 World Trade Center (74th floor) New York, N.Y. 10047	488-4874

Fund-raising — Food and non-alcoholic beverages may be sold with a permit from:

Department of Health 80 Lafayette Street New York, N.Y. 10013	566-5323

Gambling is illegal. Other merchandise such as books, plants, clothing, elephant sales, flea markets, etc., requires a license from:

The Department of Social Services Public Solicitations Section 66 Leonard Street (9th floor) New York, N.Y. 10013	553-5441 554-5442

Lighting — Licensed contractor must be used for any extensive lighting other than plug-in house circuit

Portable Rides — All portable rides need to be licensed by the Department of Consumer Affairs

Sound Device Permit — Permit needs to be obtained from the local precinct when amplified sound is used for $5.00 per day

Street Clean-up — Sprucing up the street before or after the scheduled activity is basically the responsibility of the sponsoring group. For additional help, including the possibility of extra litter baskets and manual brooms, a letter indicating planned date of activity and alternate dates should be sent at least 2 weeks before the event to:

Department of Sanitation
Community Services Office
125 Worth Street
New York, N.Y. 10013

Structures, Platforms and Bandstands — Plans for any structure which is meant to hold people need to be approved by the Department of Buildings before a Street Activity Permit is issued. No special permit is required if a flat-bed truck is used for this purpose

Flea Market Permits	566-5422
Parade Permits	374-6959
Street Peddling Permits	566-5323

Some of the major Street Fairs in New York City are (Call for dates)

In the Fall:

Feast of San Gennaro — 226-9546
140 Mulberry Street
New York, New York

One World Festival — 686-0710
35th Street and Second Avenue

Edgar Allen Poe Festival — 880-8287
on the West side

TAMA County Fair — 674-5094
Third Avenue Merchants Association
270 Third Avenue
New York, New York 10010

Third Avenue Fair — 759-9941
from 68th Street to 96th Street

Upper Eastside Street Fair — 472-1001
Our Town
500 East 82nd Street
New York, N.Y. 10028

Village Halloween Parade — 581-7217
starts at West Street

In the Spring:

Feast of St. Anthony — 777-2755
Shrine of St. Anthony
151 Thompson Street
New York, N.Y. 10012

The 52nd Street Fair — 593-3983
Madam La Farge Productions
209 West 86th Street
New York, N.Y. 10024

Lower Eastside Jewish Festival — 475-6200

Museum Mile — 860-6868
Fifth Avenue between 86th-105th Streets

Ninth Avenue Fair 581-7217
Ninth Avenue Association
400 West 50th Street
New York, N.Y. 10019

Also see: EXHIBITS: OUTDOORS
Restored Village
Snug Harbor Cultural Center

****

For GYMNASIUMS see: SCHOOLS

HOTELS

Hotel Algonquin 840-6800
59 West 44th Street
New York, N.Y. 10036
Contact: Managing Director's Office

Stratford Suite
Seating capacity: 30 in 3rd floor Stratford Suite for cocktail party
Space is traditionally known for literary and book critic functions,
 theater and press conferences

Ansonia Hotel 874-1279
2109 Broadway (btw. 73rd & 74th Streets)
New York, N.Y. 10023
Contact: The Guild Rehearsal Studios

Theater, 15 studios
Seating capacity: 75/90 in complete off-Broadway Three Muses Theater;
 30' x 18' to 35' x 40' of studio space is available
Rental fee: varies
Dance floors
Suggested uses: class, workshop, music, theater, rehearsal, dance

The Barbizon Hotel 838-5700
140 East 63rd Street
New York, N.Y. 10021
Contact: Barry Mann, General Manager

Auditorium/recital room, rehearsal space, conference room,
 small ballroom/exhibit space, reception area
Seating capacity: 200 theater/150 banquet style
Rental fee: $150 minimum plus tax
Stage, platform, piano, dance floor, kitchen; food may be served
Suggested uses: all special events are possible including recitals

Barbizon Plaza Hotel 247-7000
106 Central Park South
New York, N.Y. 10019
Contact: Charles Roarty

Auditorium/theater, rehearsal space, conference room,
　ballroom/exhibit space, reception area
Seating capacity: 505 in auditorium; 15/250 in conference room;
　15/225 for banquets; 12,000 sq. ft. of exhibition space is available
Stage, platform, piano, kitchen; space's own food only may be served
View of Central Park
Suggested uses: all special events are possible

Berkshire Place 753-5800
21 East 52nd Street (at Madison Avenue) ext. 7127
New York, N.Y. 10022
Contact: June Martinez, Banquet Manager

3 meeting rooms (The Ambassador, The Hampton, The Madison);
　2 executive board rooms
Seating capacity: 20/50 persons in meeting rooms; 10/15
　in executive board rooms
Note: This is a recently renovated Dunfey Classic Hotel

Roosevelt Hotel 661-9600
Madison Avenue & 45th Street ext. 7125
New York, N.Y. 10017
Contact: Ms. Ronnie Kirschner, Assistant Director of Sales

Terrace Room, Oval Suite, Colonial Room, Grand Ballroom,
　meeting rooms, exhibit spaces, foyer, balcony
Seating capacity: 500 theatre-style/270 classroom-style/545 banquet-style/
　600 for a reception in 86' x 48' with 23' ceiling Terrace Room; 300
　theatre-style/150 classroom-style/225 banquet-style/300 for a reception
　in 62' x 49½. Oval Suite with 23' ceiling Oval Suite; 250 banquet-style/
　425 for a reception in approximately 450 ft. x 9½' ceiling Colonial
　Room (can be divided); 1000 theatre-style/450 classroom-style/850
　banquet-style/1100 for a reception in 89' x 60' versatile Grand
　Ballroom; 300 in foyer; 30/120 in additional meeting rooms
Suggested uses: all special events are possible

Fifth Avenue Hotel 254-1300
Park Terrace Caterers, Inc.
24 Fifth Avenue
New York, N.Y. 10003
Contact: Peter Dunne, Catering Director and General Manager

Auditorium, rehearsal space, ballroom, classroom, conference room,
　exhibit space, reception area, V.I.P. suite
Seating capacity: 350 theater style/250 sitdown dinner in ballroom;
　80 theater style in V.I.P. suite
Rental fee: $750 for ballroom; $150 for V.I.P. Suite
Proscenium stage, platform, piano, dance floor, kitchen; space's
　own catered food only may be served
Suggested uses: all special events are possible including a wedding,
　bar mitzvah, fund-raiser, or fashion show, except a concert

Golden Gate Motor Inn 743-4000
3867 Shore Parkway
Brooklyn, New York
Contact: Rita or Chuck

Overlooking the water in the Sheepshead Bay Section,
   this facility offers both banquet and exhibit space
   in its multi-purpose ballroom
Guest capacity: 300
Parking available for 400 cars

Grand Hyatt New York   (212) 883-1234
150 East 42nd Street (at Grand Central Station)   (800) 228-9000
New York, N.Y. 10017
Contact: Catering Manager

30-story mirrored hotel
Regency Room on Mezzanine Level has 1400 sq. ft. and can
   accommodate 150 for a reception, 120 banquet, 180 theatre,
   80 school room and 40 conference style
20 meeting rooms are on Conference Level, 4th floor, ranging
   from 490 sq. ft. to 1260 sq. ft. with 8 ft. ceilings, accommodating
   120/315 for a reception, 50/125 banquet, 70/180 theatre, 35/90
   school room and 30/80 conference style
5 ballrooms are on Ballroom Level, 5th floor, ranging from 3,200 sq. ft.
   to 18,950 sq. ft. accommodating 800/4700 for a reception, 320/1600
   banquet, 460/2700 theatre and 225/1350 school room style
These facilities might be able to function as exhibit spaces
20 Conference Parlors are on the Parlor Level, 6th floor, which can
   accommodate 15/20 persons each conference style. Average room
   size is 12' x 26' with 10 ft. ceilings
Atrium-lobby, glass-roofed garden terrace (Garden Room)

Halloran House   755-4000
525 Lexington Avenue (btw. 48th and 49th Streets)
New York, N.Y. 10017
Contact: Banquet Manager

6 meeting rooms on the second floor can accommodate from
   32/220 school room, 50/350 banquet, 50/450 theatre and
   75/700 reception style. Smallest is 26 ft. x 24 ft. x 16 ft.;
   largest is 135 ft. x 32 ft. x 14 ft.
The Garden Room and Fountain Room on the sixteenth floor
   are 48 ft. x 39 ft. x 12 ft. and 51 ft. x 32 ft. x 12 ft. respectively.
   Garden Room can accommodate 28 school room, 50 theatre,
   90 banquet and 150 reception style; Fountain Room can accommodate
   80 school room, 100 banquet, 125 theatre and 200 reception style
Audio-visual equipment on premises

The Harley of New York   490-8900
214 East 42nd Street
New York, New York 10017
Contact: Sharon Wright, Director of Sales

793 rooms, 7 second floor meeting rooms in 40-story hotel
Seating capacity: 25/300

Holiday Inn (at the Coliseum)   581-8100
440 West 57th Street
New York, N.Y. 10019
Contact: Louis Allen, Banquet Manager

Embassy Room, Renaissance Room, Imperial Room, Mandarin Room,
Medallion Room, Marco Polo Room, Coliseum Room
Seating capacity: 1000 auditorium-style in Embassy Room and
Imperial Room (can open into one room); 300 auditorium/
260 banquet/100 classroom-style for Renaissance Room;
300 auditorium style for Imperial Room; 40 in other rooms

Hotel Overlooking Gramercy Park

Hotel Overlooking Gramercy Park   737-7536
New York, N.Y.

Auditorium, rehearsal space, lounge, conference room,
ballroom, roof garden, exhibit space
Guest capacity: 12/150 sitdown; 500 maximum cocktails
Rental fee: varies with space from $175 and up for a meeting
display, etc.
Platform, piano, dance floor, kitchen; food may be served
Suggested uses: all special events are possible except a concert or fair

Hotel Plaza

Hotel Plaza   759-7011
Fifth Avenue & 59th Street
New York, N.Y. 10019
Contact: Tim Clapp, Banquet Manager

Variously sized rooms and foyers including Grand Ballroom
Guest capacity: 700 Grand Ballroom; 20/500 in other rooms

The Palace 888-7000
Madison Avenue at 50th Street
New York, N.Y. 10020
Contact: Mal J. Seymourian, Director of Sales

3 modern meeting rooms, 3 historic meeting rooms, 2 lounges, 2 restaurants
Seating capacity: 50/150 in modern meeting rooms; 15/120 in historic meeting rooms
This new 55 story hotel with 650 rooms and suites is entered through the historic cobblestone courtyard of the 100-year-old neo-Italian Renaissance of the landmark Villard Houses, which is part of this luxury hotel

Parker Meridien New York 245-5000
West 56th Street between 6th & 7th Avenues
New York, N.Y. 10019
Contact: Sales Department

Conference rooms, banquet rooms, 8 squash and racquet ball courts, complete health club, rooftop swimming pool, jogging track
Seating capacity: 160/190 in ballroom; 145/170 in Room A; 115/130 in Room B; 40 banquet-style in Room C
Note: This 600 room, 40 story hotel is operated by Meridien, an international hotel chain and a subsidiary of Air France

Recently Restored Landmark Hotel

Recently Restored Landmark Hotel 737-7536
New York, N.Y.

An old-style hotel off Fifth Avenue in the 20's which offers both banquet and exhibit space
Guest capacity: 600 theater-style/400 sitdown with dancing/ 300 conference-style in Ballroom; 200 maximum in Georgian Room; additional smaller rooms
39 8' x 10' exhibit tables

St. Regis-Sheraton 753-4500
St. Regis Roof
Fifth Avenue and 55th Street
New York, N.Y. 10022
Contact: Vickie Durfee, Assistant Banquet Manager

Ballroom
Seating capacity: 120/550 people may be accommodated
Baroque-style, crystal chandeliered ballroom is situated on the 20th floor
Suggested uses: private parties including weddings

St. Regis Penthouse
Windowed area
Seating capacity: 30/300 people may be accommodated
  in 38' x 54' area adjacent to the St. Regis ballroom
Suggested uses: breakfast, lunch or dinner meeting, conference,
  buffet or cocktail reception, fashion show, etc. Normally used
  in conjunction with roof

Sheraton Centre 581-1000
801 Seventh Avenue (at 52nd Street)
New York, New York 10019
Contact: Sales Department

1 main ballroom, 5 smaller ballrooms, 35 meeting rooms
Seating capacity: 2400 theatre-style/3000 cocktail reception
  in main ballroom; 5 smaller ballrooms are each 3000 sq. ft.;
  meeting rooms hold 40/100
The main ballroom is one of the largest in New York City

United Nations Plaza Hotel 355-3400
One United Nations Plaza
New York, N.Y. 10017
Contact: Gloria Simons, Sales and Catering Manager

3 meeting/banquet rooms (Dag Hammarskjold, U Thant, Coffee Mill),
  party/meeting room (Ambassador Grill), lounge, swimming pool
Seating capacity: 70 classroom/120 theatre/100 banquet style in
  Dag Hammarskjold Room; 15/25 for a meeting, 50 for a banquet
  in U Thant Room; 15/25 for a meeting, 50/60 for a banquet
  in the Coffee Mill
Rental fee: varies from $100 to $500; $1,000 base price for
  swimming pool on Wednesday evening
6' x 12' platform, 5' x 5' dance floor; food may be served
Suggested uses: all special events are possible including a fashion show
  at the pool except a dance (unless rent larger floor). Limited exhibit space

Vista International New York 938-9100
3 World Trade Center
New York, N.Y. 10048
Contact: Ian Lloyd-Jones, Director of Sales

825 guest rooms. Private function facilities —
3rd floor private salons:

Theme Parties available in International Ballroom:

(a) **On The New York Waterfront in the 19th Century:** huge murals of clipperships, yard arms and sails form the backdrop of a busy quay. Amidst an authentic wharf with loading crates, barrels and bundles, a sumptuous buffet is laid out with shop fronts of yesteryear, fishmongers, bakers and butchers. A real seafaring pub dispenses wine and ale. Period costumed waiters and waitresses, etc.

(b) **Nostalgic Subway Champagne Soiree:** a 1922 vintage subway in mint condition, with waiters dressed in black tie and tails serving chilled champagne takes guests on half-hour ride to Brooklyn Transit Museum for a sumptuous buffet amidst period subway cars.

(c) **A Salute To The "Good Ole U.S.A.":** a Virginia Smokehouse, a Mississippi Riverboat and a Pennsylvania Dutch Farm House are used to create a setting for food displays from these regions, as does the Covered Wagon of the 1800's and a chandeliered gazebo of the Roaring Twenties. Waiters and waitresses costumed in period style and entertainment from a variety of states and times.

* * * * * * *

LIBRARIES

The New York Public Library
Branch Library System
Office of The Branch Libraries
8 East 40th Street
New York, New York 10016

930-0842

The New York Public Library has 82 branches in Manhattan, The Bronx, and Staten Island. A number of the larger libraries have auditoriums and almost all have some form of meeting space, often the Children's Room, available for meetings during non-service hours. A selected list of branch facilities follows.

Rental fee: A nominal fee is charged; for information, consult the branch librarian. All meetings must be without fee to the public and be related to a cultural, educational or civic purpose.

The brochure "It's Your Library" lists the names and addresses of all 82 branch libraries and may be requested at the above address, or at any of the branches.

MANHATTAN BRANCH LIBRARIES

Aguilar, 174 E. 110th St.   534-2930
Seating capacity: 40

Bloomingdale, 150 W. 100th St.   222-8030
Seating capacity: 85

Chatham Square, 33 E. Broadway   964-6598
Seating capacity: 60

Columbus, 742 Tenth Ave.   586-5098
Seating capacity: 50

Countee Cullen, 104 W. 136th St.   281-0700
Seating capacity: 120

Donnell Library Ctr., 20 W. 53rd St.   621-0614
Seating capacity: 278

Fifty-eighth Street, 127 E. 58th St.   759-7358
Seating capacity: 50

George Bruce, 518 W. 125th St.   662-9727
Seating capacity: 75

Hamilton Fish Park, 415 E. Houston St.   673-2290
Seating capacity: 62

Hamilton Grange, 503 W. 145th St.   926-2147
Seating capacity: 61

Harlem, 9 W. 125th St.   348-5620
Seating capacity: 75

Hudson Park, 10 Seventh Ave. South   243-6876
Seating capacity: 105

Inwood, 4790 Broadway   942-2445
Seating capacity: 110

Jefferson Market, 425 Ave. of Americas   243-4334
Seating capacity: 70

Kips Bay, 446 Third Ave.   683-2520
Seating capacity: 40

Library & Museum of
The Performing Arts at Lincoln Ctr.   799-2200
Seating capacity: 212

Muhlenberg, 209 W. 23rd St.   924-1585
Seating capacity: 60

115th Street, 203 W. 115th St.   666-9393
Seating capacity: 74

125th Street, 224 E. 125th St.   534-5050
Seating capacity: 50

St. Agnes, 444 Amsterdam Ave.   877-4380
Seating capacity: 50

Tompkins Square, 331 E. 10th Street   228-4747
Seating capacity: 74

Washington Heights,
   1000 St. Nicholas Avenue   923-6054
Seating capacity: 140

Yorkville, 222 E. 79th St.   744-5824
Seating capacity: 74

Also see — New York Public Library,
   42nd Street Branch

BRONX BRANCH LIBRARIES

Allerton, 2740 Barnes Ave.   881-4240
Seating capacity: 74

Baychester, 2049 Asch Loop North   379-6700
Seating capacity: 60

Clason's Point, 1215 Morrison Ave.   842-1235
Seating capacity: 50

Edenwald, 1255 E. 233rd St.   798-3355
Seating capacity: 60

Fordham Library Center,
   2556 Bainbridge Ave.   220-6572
Seating capacity: 70
(including Bronx Reference Center)

Francis Martin, 2150 University Ave.   295-5287
Seating capacity: 70

Grand Concourse, 155 E. 173rd St.   583-6611
Seating capacity: 62

High Bridge, 78 W. 168th St.   293-7800
Seating capacity: 45

Hunt's Point, 877 Southern Blvd.   542-2996
Seating capacity: 72

Jerome Park, 118 Eames Pl.   549-5200
Seating capacity: 49

Kingsbridge, 280 W. 231st St.   548-5656
Seating capacity: 45

Morrisania, 610 E. 169th St.   589-9268
Seating capacity: 40

Mosholu, 285 E. 205th St.   882-8239
Seating capacity: 64

Mott Haven, 321 E. 140th St.   665-4878
Seating capacity: 74

Pelham Bay, 3060 Middletown Rd.   792-6744
Seating capacity: 60

Riverdale, 5540 Mosholu Ave.   549-1212
Seating capacity: 100

Soundview, 660 Soundview Ave.   589-0880
Seating capacity: 60

Throg's Neck, 3025 Cross Bronx
   Expressway Extension   792-2612
Seating capacity: 40

Tremont, 1866 Washington Ave.   299-5177
Seating capacity: 125

Wakefield, 4100 Lowerre Place   652-4663
Seating capacity: 75

West Farms, 2085 Honeywell Ave.   367-5376
Seating capacity: 90

Westchester Square, 2521 Glebe Ave.   863-0436
Seating capacity: 50

STATEN ISLAND BRANCH LIBRARIES

Dongan Hills, 1617 Richmond Rd.   351-1444
Seating capacity: 60

Great Kills, 56 Giffords Lane   984-6670
Seating capacity: 40

New Dorp, 309 New Dorp Lane   351-2977
Seating capacity: 49

Port Richmond, 75 Bennett St.   442-0158
Seating capacity: 70

Prince's Bay, 6054 Amboy Rd.   356-1130
Seating capacity: 20

St. George Library Ctr., 10 Hyatt St.   442-8560
Seating capacity: 85

Stapleton, 132 Canal St.   727-0427
Seating capacity: 60

Todt Hill-Westerleigh,
   1891 Victory Blvd.   442-8373
Seating capacity: 30

Tottenville, 7430 Amboy Rd.   984-0945
Seating capacity: 30

West New Brighton, 976 Castleton Ave.   442-1416
Seating capacity: 75

Brooklyn Public Library   **636-3111**
Grand Army Plaza
Brooklyn, N.Y. 11238
Contact: Ellen Rudley, Public Relations

The Brooklyn Public Library System administers 57 branch libraries in Brooklyn.
   A brochure listing names and locations of these libraries may be requested
at the Central Library, Grand Army Plaza, or at any of the local branches.
There is no rental fee.

BROOKLYN BRANCH LIBRARIES

Arlington, 203 Arlington Ave.
   at Warwick St.   277-0160
Seating capacity: 36

Bay Ridge, 7223 Ridge Blvd.
   at 73rd St.   748-3042
Seating capacity: 100

Bedford, 496 Franklin Ave.
   at Hancock St.   638-9544
Seating capacity: 50

Borough Park, 1265 43rd St.
   near 13th Avenue   435-3375
Seating capacity: 100

Brighton Beach, 16 Brighton First Rd.
   near Brighton Beach Ave.   266-0005
Seating capacity: 45

Brooklyn Heights, 280 Cadman Plaza
   West at Clinton St.   522-4075
Seating capacity: 150

Brower Park, 725 St. Mark's Ave.
near Nostrand Ave. 778-6262
Seating capacity: 50

Brownsville, 61 Glenmore Ave.
at Watkins St. 345-1212
Seating capacity: 45

Bushwick, 340 Bushwick Ave.
at Seigel St. 443-1078
Seating capacity: 60

Canarsie, 1580 Rockaway Pkwy.
near Avenue J 257-2180
Seating capacity: 50

Carroll Gardens, 396 Clinton St.
at Union St. 625-5838
Seating capacity: 100 & 45 (2 separate)

Clinton Hill, 380 Washington Ave.
near Lafayette Ave. 857-8038
Seating capacity: 50

Coney Island, 1901 Mermaid Ave.
at West 19th St. 266-1121
Seating capacity: 80

Crown Heights, 560 New York Ave.
at Maple St. 773-1223
Seating capacity: 50

Cypress Hills, 465 Fountain Ave.
near Hegeman Ave. 277-8257
Seating capacity: 35

DeKalb, 784 Bushwick Ave.
at DeKalb Ave. 452-5678
Seating capacity: 100

Dyker, 8202 13th Ave.
at 82nd St. 748-1395
Seating capacity: 50

Eastern Parkway, 1044 Eastern
Parkway at Schenectady Ave. 756-5150
Seating capacity: 50

Flatbush, 22 Linden Blvd.
near Flatbush Ave. 282-2017
Seating capacity: 50

Flatlands, 2065 Flatbush Ave.
at Avenue P 252-6115
Seating capacity: 50

Gravesend, 303 Avenue X
near West 2nd St. 376-9311
Seating capacity: 50

Greenpoint, 107 Norman Ave.
at Leonard St. 383-6692
Seating capacity: 50

Highlawn, 1664 West 13th St.
at Kings Highway 837-1700
Seating capacity: 50

Homecrest, 2525 Coney Island Ave.
near Avenue V 645-2727
Seating capacity: 50

Jamaica Bay, 9727 Sea View Ave.
at East 98th Street 531-1602
Seating capacity: 50

Kensington, 410 Ditmas Ave.
near East Fifth St. 436-0525
Seating capacity: 50

Kings Bay, 3650 Nostrand Ave.
near Avenue W 332-5656
Seating capacity: 50

Kings Highway, 2115 Ocean Ave.
near Kings Highway 375-3037
Seating capacity: 100

Leonard, 81 Devoe St.
at Leonard St. 387-3800
Seating capacity: 75

Macon, 361 Lewis Ave.
at Macon St. 453-3333
Seating capacity: 50

Mapleton, 1702 60th St.
at 17th Ave. 232-0346
Seating capacity: 100

Marcy, 617 DeKalb Ave.
near Nostrand Ave. 858-1878
Seating capacity: 50

McKinley Park, 6802 Fort Hamilton
Parkway at 68th St. 748-5800
Seating capacity: 60

Midwood, 975 East 16th St.
near Avenue J 377-7972
Seating capacity: 100

Mill Basin, 2385 Ralph Ave.
at Avenue N 763-8700
Seating capacity: 50

New Lots, 665 New Lots Ave.
at Barbey St 649-3700
Seating capacity: 110

New Utrecht, 1743 86th St.
at Bay 17th St. 236-4086
Seating capacity: 116

Pacific, 25 Fourth Ave.
at Pacific St. 638-5180
Seating capacity: 50

Paerdegat, 850 East 59th St.
near Flatlands Ave. 763-4848
Seating capacity: 50

Red Hook, 7 Wolcott St.
at Dwight St. 875-4412
Seating capacity: 50

Rugby, 1000 Utica Ave.
  near Tilden Ave. 345-9264
Seating capacity: 45

Ryder, 5902 23rd Ave.
  at 59th St. 232-5064
Seating capacity: 50

Saratoga, 8 Hopkinson Ave.
  at Macon St. 455-3078
Seating capacity: 50

Sheepshead Bay, 2636 E. 14th St.
  near Avenue Z 743-0663
Seating capacity: 50

Spring Creek, 12143 Flatlands Ave.
  at New Jersey 649-0020
Seating capacity: 50

Sunset Park, 5108 Fourth Ave.
  at 51st St. 439-8846
Seating capacity: 50

Ulmer Park, 2602 Bath Ave.
  at 26th Ave. 266-7373
Seating capacity: 50

Walt Whitman, 93 St. Edwards St.
  at Auburn Pl. 855-1508
Seating capacity: 50

Washington Irving, 360 Irving Ave.
  at Woodbine St. 386-6212
Seating capacity: 50

Williamsburgh, 240 Division Ave.
  at Marcy Ave. 782-4600
Seating capacity: 100

Windsor Terrace, 160 E. Fifth St.
  at Fort Hamilton Pl. 853-7265
Seating capacity: 50

Central Library (Ingersoll Building), Grand Army Plaza
Seating capacity: Auditorium — 100; Conference Room 214 — 30

Queens Borough Public Library **990-0700**
89-11 Merrick Boulevard
Jamaica, N.Y. 11432
Contact: Director's Office

Auditorium, 2 meeting rooms
Seating capacity: 200 in auditorium; 50 in each of the meeting rooms
  which can be joined into one
Rental fee: none during regular library hours; $5.00 per hour
  after regular hours
Stage, platform, P.A. system

Queens Borough Public Library has 57 branches, most of which
  have meeting room facilities. Information on names and
  locations of these libraries as well as regulations governing
  the use of their facilities may be obtained at the above
  address or at any of the branches in Queens.

QUEENS BRANCH LIBRARIES

Arverne, 312 Beach Ave. & 54th St. 634-4784
Seating capacity: 30

Astoria, 14-01 Astoria Blvd., L.I.C. 278-0601
Seating capacity: 50/200

Auburndale, 25-55 Francis Lewis
  Blvd., Flushing 352-2027
Seating capacity: 50

Baisley Park, 117-11 Sutphin Blvd.,
  Jamaica 529-1590
Seating capacity: 50

Bay Terrace, 18-36 Bell Blvd.,
  Flushing 423-7004
Seating capacity: 50

Bellerose, 250-06 Hillside Ave. 343-0303
Seating capacity: 50

Briarwood, 138-12 84th Rd. 658-1680
Seating capacity: 50

Broadway, 40-20 Broadway, L.I.C. 721-2462
Seating capacity: 100

Cambria Heights, 220-20 Linden Blvd.   528-3535
Seating capacity: 25

Corona, 41-08 102nd St.   426-2844
Seating capacity: 30

Douglaston, 249-01 Northern Blvd.,
 Little Neck   229-0590
Seating capacity: 55

East Elmhurst, 95-06 Astoria Blvd.,
 E. Elmhurst   424-2619
Seating capacity: 50

East Flushing, 196-36 Northern Blvd.,
 Flushing   357-6643
Seating capacity: 50

Elmhurst, 86-01 Broadway   271-1020
Seating capacity: 200

Far Rockaway, 16-37 Central Ave.   327-2549
Seating capacity: 50

Flushing, 41-25 Main St.   445-0800
Seating capacity: 165

Forest Hills, 108-19 71st Ave.   268-7934
Seating capacity: Auditorium—100;
 Children's room—50

Fresh Meadows, 193-20 Horace
 Harding Expressway   454-7272
Seating capacity: 55

Glen Oaks, 256-04 Union Turnpike   347-8200
Seating capacity: Auditorium—50;
 Children's Room—50

Glendale, 78-60 73rd Pl.   821-4980
Seating capacity: 80

Hillcrest, 187-05 Union Turnpike   454-2786
Seating capacity: 50

Hollis, 1202-05 Hillside Ave.   465-7355
Seating capacity: 50

Howard Beach, 92-06 156th Ave.   641-7086
Seating capacity: 50

Jackson Heights, 35-51 81st St.   899-2500
Seating capacity: 80 in auditorium;
 70 in children's room

Laurelton, 134-26 225th St.   528-2822
Seating capacity: 50

Lefferts Reference Center,
 103-34 Lefferts Boulevard   843-5950
Seating capacity: 50

Lefrak City, 98-25 Horace Harding
 Expressway   592-0266
Seating capacity: 50

Maspeth, 69-70 Grand Ave.   639-5228
Seating capacity: 50

McGoldrick, 155-06 Roosevelt Ave.,
 Flushing   353-0839

Middle Village, 75-30 Metropolitan Ave.   326-1390
Seating capacity: 25

Mitchell-Linden, 29-42 Union St.,
 Flushing   539-2330
Seating capacity: 40

Ozone Park, 92-24 Rockaway Blvd.,
 Rockaway Beach   845-3127
Seating capacity: 100

Peninsula, 92-25 Rockaway Blvd.,
 Rockaway Beach   634-0101
Seating capacity: 100

Pomonok, 158-21 Jewel Ave.,
 Flushing   591-4343
Seating capacity: 50

Queens Village, 94-11 217th St.   776-6800
Seating capacity: 120

Rego Park, 91-41 63rd Drive   459-5140
Seating capacity: 50

Ridgewood, 20-12 Madison St.   821-4770
Seating capacity: 80

Rochdale Village, 169-09 137th Ave.,
 Jamaica   723-4440
Seating capacity: 50

St. Albans, 187-10 Linden Blvd.,
 Jamaica   528-8196
Seating capacity: 50

Seaside, 116-15 Rockaway Beach Blvd.   634-1876
Seating capacity: 50

South Hollis, 204-01 Hollis Ave.,
 Jamaica   465-6779
Seating capacity: 50

South Ozone Park, 128-16 Rockaway
 Blvd.   529-1660
Seating capacity: 50

Steinway, 21-45 31st St., L.I.C.   728-1965
Seating capacity: Auditorium—125;
 Children's room—75

Sunnyside, 43-06 Greenpoint Ave.,
 L.I.C.   784-3033
Seating capacity: 45

Vleigh, 72-33 Vleigh Place, Flushing   261-6654
Seating capacity: 50

Whitestone, 151-10 14th Rd.   767-8010
Seating capacity: 50

Windsor Park, 79-50 Bell Blvd.,
 Bayside   468-8300
Seating capacity: 70

Woodhaven, 85-41 Forest Parkway   849-1010   Woodside, 54-22 Skillman Avenue   429-4700
Seating capacity: 75   Seating capacity: 75

Also see: Private Parties/Public Places

* * * * * * *

Avant-garde Art Gallery   737-7536
New York, New York

3,000 sq. ft. of open space plus banquet room on floor below.
Located in Tribeca, one block from City Hall, this
   large facility features the work of experimental artists
   and is one of the few art galleries to welcome private parties.
Accommodates approximately 350 guests
The Greek restaurant on street floor will cater, or provide
   your own food service

Avant-garde Art Gallery

The Drawing Center   982-5266
137 Greene Street
New York, N.Y. 10012
Contact: Martha Beck or Marie Keller

Lecture space
Seating capacity: 200
Suggested uses: concert, class, lecture, meeting, performance
Note: Smoking and food are not allowed

Fifth Avenue Loft with Tree-Top View of Historic Park

Fifth Avenue Loft With A Tree-top View of Historic Park   (212) 737-7536
New York, New York

Overlooks Madison Square Park & Flatiron Building.
Located in building designed by Stanford White. Suitable
   for seminars, classes, workshops and private parties for
   up to 60 people. Abundant natural light. Custom
catering and appropriate music (live and recorded) available.

A Homey Loft in Tribeca   737-7536
New York, New York

2,200 sq. ft. available for quiet parties and weddings.
   Furnished comfortably with antiques and homey touches.
Entertainment and sound system available.
Guest capacity: 150 maximum

Jazz Loft on West 27th Street   737-7536
New York, New York

Seating capacity: 100 livingroom style
Stage large enough for 10-piece band; raised platform,
   dance floor, stage lighting, fireplace, P.A. system, Bass amps,
   drums, bar; food may be served
Suggested uses: concert, lecture, party, performance, reception
Note: Space is available days and evenings during the week
   except Thursday-Sunday evenings

K & K Space And Toy Company, Inc.   267-5756
146 Chambers Street
New York, New York 10007
Contact: Deborah Kein or E. Jan Kounitz

Multi-purpose studio
Seating capacity: 74 for a performance
Rental fee: negotiable
Piano, lighting plot, dimmer board, dance floor; food may be served
Suggested uses: all special events are possible including a reading,
   videotaping, photography and exhibit of 2-dimensional art work

A Loft for Musical Functions   737-7536
Brooklyn, New York

Brick walls, natural wood floor, tiered cushioned seating
   along wall, butcher block bar; relaxed musical atmosphere
Guest capacity: 120 maximum
Light dinners may be served
Suggested uses: musical showcases, jazz workshops, recordings, etc.

Loft With Three Skylights   737-7536
New York, New York

Seating capacity: 150 for cocktails; 100 buffet style;
   45/50 sitdown dinner
Mirrored fireplace, kitchen alcove
Situated in a 100-year-old reconverted 2-story building
   in the West 30's owned by a plant design consultant. Loft
   is permeated with a soft milk light due to its three skylights
   and white/beige coloring throughout.
Food may be served
Suggested uses: private party, including a wedding, reception,
   fashion photography

Studio of Creative Movement 243-7758
60 West 25th Street
New York, N.Y. 10010
Contact: Merle Lister

Rehearsal space, conference room
Seating capacity: approximately 100
Piano, dance floor
Suggested uses: concert, class, lecture, meeting, theater performance, poetry reading, dance

Studio 505 431-7748
39 Walker Street (top floor)
New York, N.Y. 10013
Contact: Marc Kaczmarek

Loft space
Seating capacity: approximately 45' x 45' sq. ft. of space is available
Light refreshments may be served
Suggested uses: dance, photography, Tai Chi and other workshops

Studio We 260-1211
193 Eldridge Street
New York, N.Y. 10002
Contact: James Duboise

Loft space, recording studio
Seating capacity: 100
Rental fee: negotiable, usually $5.00 per hour
Stage, platform, piano, bass amp, drums; food may be served

Versatile Dance/Rehearsal Loft

Versatile Dance/Rehearsal Loft on West 21st Street 737-7536
New York, New York

Theatre/rehearsal space, reception area
Seating capacity: 99 for theatre/dance; 175 classroom-style; 5,000 sq. ft. of studio space is available
Dancers' floor
Rental fee: negotiable
Piano, sound and lighting system, well equipped kitchen/lounge; catering is available or bring your own
Suggested uses: dance recital, lecture, meeting, theatrical performance, workshop, casting call, TV commercial, photography
Note: Extended long-term use is negotiable

Also see: PRIVATE PARTIES/PRIVATE PLACES

MEETING ROOMS/CONFERENCE ROOMS/AUDITORIUMS

(Seating 499 or less)

American Arbitration Association	10/30
Exhibition/Hospitality Railroad Car	40
Academic Review	5/50
George Morrison Studios	50
Cooking Center in the West 30's	40/60
Tibet Center	50/60
Museum of Broadcasting	63
American Association of University Women	30/70
Mechanics Institute	20/70
Mercantile Library	20/70
Gateway National Recreation Area	25/80
Queens Museum	65/80
Morris-Jumel Mansion	20/90
East Side International Community Center	35/100
Eastern Christian Leasing Center	100
Fraunces Tavern Museum	100
Hartley House	100
La Guardia Memorial House	50/100
Margaret Sanger Center	25/100
Willkie Memorial Building	100
Center for Inter-American Relations	15/110
Hughes Hall	115
Anthroposophical Society of America	120
East/West Center for Holistic Health	100/125
Gimbel's East	125
Sam & Esther Minskoff Cultural Center	25/125
New York Academy of Sciences	20/125
Restored Village	125
Waterside Swim & Health Club	125
Women's City Club of New York, Inc.	20/125
Catholic Kolping Society	50/130
Wave Hill Center for Environmental Studies	48/130
Cultural Affairs Department	100/150
Langston Hughes Community Library and Cultural Center	150
Metropolis Roller Skate Club	150
Riverdale-Yonkers Society for Ethical Culture	150
Sky Rink	150
John Andrew Spaulding's Jazz Gallery	100/175
Mosholu-Montefiore Community Center	150/175
Seamen's Church Institute	25/175
Educational Alliance	200
Flushing Jewish Center	25/200
Harkness House	50/200
Jewish Museum	200
Metropolitan Republican Club	35/200
William Sobelson Associates	20/200
New York Genealogical & Biographical Society	60/210
Jewish Community Center of Yonkers	125/225
George Tomov Studio	225
Hudson Guild	10/240
Oval Room	30/230
Faculty House	10/250
Jewish Guild for the Blind	250
Lenox Hill Neighborhood Association	15/250
Salem Community Service Council, Inc.	250
Studio 58 Playhouse, Inc.	250
Frederick Douglass Community Center	275
Phipps Central Harlem Center	287
Bard Hall	100/300
Drew Hamilton C.Y.O Community Center	25/300
Harlem State Office Building	20/300
New York Blood Center	40/348
Brooklyn Botanic Garden	350
Workmen's Circle Building	12/350
Jewish Center of Bayside Hills	35/385
District 1199	150/450
Manhattanville Community Centers, Inc.	75/450

Also see: CHURCHES
CONFERENCE CENTERS
HOTELS
LIBRARIES
LOFTS
PERFORMANCE SPACES (Concert/Recital)
PERFORMANCE SPACES (Dance/Theatre)
SCHOOLS
Y's

The Faculty House, Columbia University

Academic Review 724-6011
3 West 73rd Street
New York, N.Y. 10023
Contact: Les Halpert, Educational Services Director

Classroom, conference room, meeting room
Seating capacity: 5/50
Rental fee: varies with function and number of people
Kitchen; food may be served
Suggested uses: class, lecture, meeting

The American Arbitration Association 484-3200
140 West 51st Street
New York, N.Y. 10020
Contact: Ms. Duffy

13 conference rooms
Seating capacity: 10/30
Rental fee: $85 to $150 per day depending on room
Suggested uses: class, lecture, meeting, conference, hearing
Note: Space is only available during the day Monday through Friday

The American Association of University Women 684-6068
New York City Branch, Inc.
111 East 37th Street
New York, N.Y. 10016
Contact: Executive Secretary, 9 a.m. to 1 p.m.

Meeting rooms, patio
Seating capacity: 70 upstairs; 30 downstairs
Kitchen; food may be served
Space is a brownstone
Suggested uses: meeting, small wedding reception

Anthroposophical Society of America 685-4618
211 Madison Avenue (btw. 35th & 36th Streets)
New York, N.Y. 10016
Contact: Mona Jane Keimig

Auditorium, rehearsal space, conference room, exhibit space
Seating capacity: 120
Rental fee: negotiable
Stage, platform, piano; refreshments may be served
Space is in a former carriage house

Bard Hall 694-6853
50 Haven Avenue
New York, N.Y. 10032
Contact: Beryl Wright, Assistant to the Manager

Rehearsal space, classroom, conference room, exhibit space,
    reception area, lounge/meeting rooms, dining room, gymnasium,
    outdoor terrace, grill room
Seating capacity: 250 in 10' x 20' lounge; 100/200 on terrace;
    300 in solarium
Rental fee: $200 for main lounge; $100 for 11th floor lounge;
    $100 for grill room
20' portable stage, piano, fireplace, dance floor, kitchen;
    food may be served
View of the Hudson River and the George Washington Bridge
Suggested uses: all special events are possible except a professional dance

Bronx House 792-1800
990 Pelham Parkway South
Bronx, N.Y. 10461
Contact: Nathan Kolodney, Executive Director

Auditorium, rehearsal space, conference room, roof garden,
 lounge, meeting rooms, gymnasium, swimming pool
Seating capacity: 350/400
Rental fee: varies with function
Stage, platform, piano, dance floor, motion picture projector,
 PA system, kitchen; kosher or dairy food only may be served

Catholic Kolping Society 369-6647
165 East 88th Street
New York, N.Y. 10028
Contact: Manager

Auditorium, beer hall
Seating capacity: 130 in auditorium; 50/60 in beer hall
Stage, piano, dance floor; food may be served
Suggested uses: all special events are possible except a fair or promotion

Center for Inter-American Relations 249-8950
680 Park Avenue (at 68th Street)
New York, N.Y. 10021
Contact: Bea Wolfe

Conference room, reception area
Seating capacity: 15/110
Rental fee: varies with space used
Platform, piano, kitchen; food may be served
Suggested uses: banquet, concert, lecture, meeting, reception
Note: Space is only available to groups having an inter-American
 purpose

Cooking Center in the West 30's

Cooking Center in the West 30's 737-7536
New York, N.Y.

Two floors of a spanking new modern cooking school
 centrally located in mid-Manhattan where the restaurant
 facility is available for meetings, dinners, etc.
Seating capacity: 40 sitdown/60 buffet
Rental fee: $50 per hour for restaurant dining room; $25 per hour
 for each kitchen (includes use of all equipment)

Department of Cultural Affairs 974-1150
2 Columbus Circle (at 58th Street)
New York, N.Y. 10019
Contact: Ruth Burrell Brown

Auditorium, meeting room
Seating capacity: 150 in downstairs auditorium; 100 in
   9th floor meeting room
Rental fee: $15 an hour during the day, $135.00 an hour
   during the evening for non-profit groups for meeting room;
     $15.00 an hour plus $125.00 surcharge to keep building
   open on weekends, 8 hour minimum at $135.00 per hour for
   profit-making groups for meeting room
Food may be served by caterer of your choice
Meeting room is the former restaurant/lounge of the
   Huntington Hartford Museum which overlooks Central Park.
   Gallery space also available.

East Side International Community Center, Inc. 371-8604
931 First Avenue (at 51st Street)
New York, N.Y. 10022
Contact: Rosemarie Lombardi or Caroline Newell

Rehearsal space, multi-purpose reception area, meeting rooms,
   playground, gymnasium
Seating capacity: 100 in reception area; 35/40 in meeting rooms
Rental fee: $75 for reception area until 10 p.m., plus $20 per hour
   after 10 p.m.; $40 for meeting rooms on same time schedule.
   Negotiable over 100 people
Dance floor, kitchen; food may be served
Space used to be a public school
Suggested uses: auction, concert, class, fair, lecture, meeting,
   party, performance, reception

East/West Center for Holistic Health 673-8200
141 Fifth Avenue (btw. 20th & 21st Streets, 8th floor)
New York, N.Y. 10010
Contact: Marie Valenta, Director or Lynne Burton, Operations Manager

Classroom/meeting room, 3 conference rooms, exhibit space,
   reception area
Seating capacity: 125 in classroom/meeting room; 100 in
   large conference room
Rental fee: $75 for classroom/meeting room for 3 hours,
   $15 per hour thereafter; $75 for large conference room
   for 3 hours, $15 per hour thereafter; $50 for small conference
   room for 3 hours, $10 per hour thereafter
Dance floor, kitchen; food may be served
Suggested uses: all special events are possible except a
   professional dance or a promotion
Note: Smoking is not allowed

Faculty House 737-7536
Columbia University
New York, N.Y.

Three floors of individually furnished meeting rooms
Guest capacity: 8/250
Breakfast, lunch or dinner may be served

Flushing Jewish Center 358-7071
43-00 71st Street
Flushing, N.Y. 11358
Contact: Ed Seligman or office

Auditorium, rehearsal space, conference room, ballroom, classrooms
Seating capacity: 200 in auditorium; 600 in ballroom;
   25 in classrooms
Stage, platform, piano, dance floor
Suggested uses: all special events are possible except a fair

Fraunces Tavern Museum 425-1778
54 Pearl Street
New York, N.Y. 10004
Contact: Mary Stiles, Public Information Officer

Auditorium, conference room/exhibit space
Seating capacity: 100
Cocktails may be served
Space is in a converted sail loft building and is part of museum complex
Suggested uses: concert, lecture, meeting, party
Note: Space is not available on weekends

Frederick Douglass Community Center 865-6337
885 Columbus Avenue
New York, N.Y. 10025
Contact: Herman Bagley, Director, or Francis Cave

Auditorium/gymnasium
Seating capacity: approximately 275
Rental fee: negotiable
Stage, piano, motion picture projector

George Morrison Studios 594-2614
212 West 29th Street
New York, N.Y. 10001
Contact: David Cohen

Rehearsal space, conference room
Seating capacity: 60' x 25' of space is available in rehearsal space;
   50 in conference room
Rental fee: $7.00 per hour
Theatrical lighting

George Tomov Studio 243-6338
19 Union Square West, 6th floor
New York, New York 10003
Contact: George Tomov, Owner

Rehearsal space, classroom, conference room, exhibit space,
   reception area
Seating capacity: 225
Rental fee: $10 per hour from 8:00 a.m. to 5:30 p.m.
Piano, dance floor; food may be served
Suggested uses: all special events are possible except an auction,
   banquet or fair

Gimbel's East 348-2300
125 East 86th Street
New York, N.Y. 10028
Contact: Management Office

Auditorium
Seating capacity: 125
Restaurant; food may be served
Suggested uses: class, exhibit, lecture, meeting

Harlem State Office Building   678-2465
163 West 125th Street   678-2466
New York, N.Y. 10027   678-2467
Contact: Keith F. Hercules, Building Manager or
   Anderson McLucas, Catering Manager

Conference room, meeting rooms, exhibit space, plaza area
Seating capacity: 20/300
Piano; catered food may be served
Suggested uses: exhibit, lecture, conference, meeting, fashion show

Hartley House   246-9885
413 West 46th Street
New York, N.Y. 10036
Contact: G. Scott Milnor, Associate Director

Auditorium, classroom, conference room, reception area, gymnasium
Seating capacity: 100
Rental fee: $30 to $60
Stage, platform, piano, kitchen
Suggested uses: all special events are possible except a
   professional dance, exhibit or fair

Hudson Guild   760-9808
441 West 26th Street
New York, N.Y. 10001
Contact: Dorothy Bond, Office Manager

Auditorium, rehearsal space, conference room, meeting rooms,
   exhibit space, reception area
Seating capacity: 139 in auditorium; 240 in reception area;
   10/50 in meeting rooms
Rental fee: varies with space and time
Suggested uses: all special events are possible except a fair,
   promotion, wedding or religious ceremony

Hughes Hall
National Conference for Christians & Jews
43 West 57th Street
New York, N.Y. 10019
Contact: Mrs. Cole

Hall
Seating capacity: 115
Small stage; refreshments may be served by caterer of your choice
Suggested uses: meeting, workshop
Note: Group must have an educational or civic purpose
   and apply in writing

Jewish Center of Bayside Hills   225-5301
211th Street & 48th Avenue   224-0695
Bayside, N.Y. 11364   (after 5 p.m.)
Contact: Dave Foreman

Auditorium/ballroom, conference room, exhibit space, 3 classrooms
Seating capacity: 300 sitdown /200 ballroom-style in auditorium;
   350/385 in conference room; 35 in each classroom
Stage, piano, dance floor, 2 kitchens; kosher food only may be served
Suggested uses: all special events are possible
Note: Space is only available to non-profit groups

Jewish Community Center of Yonkers (914) 963-8457
122 South Broadway
Yonkers, N.Y. 10701
Contact: James Burke, Administrative Supervisor

Auditorium/exhibit space, theatre, classrooms/meeting rooms
Seating capacity: 225 in auditorium; 125 in theatre;
   20/60 in classrooms
Stage, piano, kitchen; kosher food only may be served
Suggested uses: meeting, etc.
Note: Space is closed on Saturdays

Jewish Guild for the Blind 595-2000
15 West 65th Street
New York, N.Y. 10023
Contact: Alan R. Morse

Auditorium
Seating capacity: 250 (flexible seating; may be partitioned
   for smaller space)
Note: Space is only available to non-profit groups and only during the day

The Jewish Museum 860-1888
1109 Fifth Avenue (at 92nd Street)
New York, N.Y. 10028
Contact: Kay Gutfreund

Auditorium (Gallery 5), Italian Room (Gallery 6)
Seating capacity: 200 in auditorium; 50/100 in Italian Room
Rental fee: $300 during museum hours (includes interpretive guide);
   $600 off-hours and during the evening
Stage, platform, PA system, kosher food and beverages only may be served
Suggested uses: luncheon, afternoon tea, dinner meeting
Note: Space is only available to groups using museum collections
   as part of their special event

Langston Hughes Community Library and Cultural Center 651-1100
102-09 Northern Boulevard 651-1101
Corona, N.Y. 11368
Contact: Anne S. Parker or Andrew Jackson, Supervisor

Auditorium/exhibit space
Seating capacity: 150
Rental fee: none during hours when open
Stage, kitchen; food may be served
Suggested use: meeting
Note: Space is only available to community groups

Lenox Hill Neighborhood Association 744-5022
321 East 70th Street
New York, N.Y. 10021
Contact: Steven Rosenberg

Auditorium, small conference rooms, gymnasium, swimming pool
Seating capacity: 250 in auditorium; 15/25 in each conference room;
  400 in gymnasium
Rental fee: by contribution
Note: Space is only available to non-profit groups. Neighborhood
  groups are welcome

Manhattanville Community Centers, Inc.　　　　　　　　　　281-5100
530 West 133rd Street
New York, N.Y. 10027
Contact: Yvonne Burroughs

Auditorium/gymnasium, rehearsal space, conference room
Seating capacity: 450 in auditorium; 75/100 in conference room
Stage, piano, dance floor, kitchen; food may be served

Margaret Sanger Center　　　　　　　　　　677-6474
380 Second Avenue (at 22nd Street)
New York, N.Y. 10010
Contact: Peter Purdy, Associate Executive Director
  of Planned Parenthood of New York City

Conference center, community room, board room
Seating capacity: 100 in 5th floor conference center (movable
  doors, can be partitioned into 4 rooms); approximately 50
  in community room; 25 in board room
Rental fee: $125 for the conference center during the day;
  $40 for board room; evening use is additional
Audio-visual equipment, drop screen, stove, bleachers
Note: Space is located in a 10-story office building which closes at 10:00 p.m.

Mechanics Institute　　　　　　　　　　840-7648
20 West 44th Street
New York, N.Y. 10035
Contact: John McCormick

Various sized classroom space
Seating capacity: up to 70
Rental fee: by donation
Note: This facility is open four days a week, Mondays through Thursdays,
  including evening hours. No smoking, no food service. Closed during July

Mercantile Library Association　　　　　　　　　　755-6710
17 East 47th Street
New York, N.Y. 10017
Contact: Claire Roth

Lecture/library room
Seating capacity: 65
Suggested uses: class, lecture, meeting, reception
Note: Space is only available in the early evening

Metropolitan Republican Club　　　　　　　　　　288-8606
122 East 83rd Street
New York, N.Y. 10028
Contact: Susan Cooper or Carmen Steele

Auditorium, rehearsal space/conference room, exhibit space
Seating capacity: 200 in auditorium; 35 in conference room
Rental fee: varies with space and time
Platform, kitchen; food may be served
Suggested uses: auction, class, exhibit, fair, lecture, meeting, party, reception

Sam & Esther Minskoff Cultural Center 737-6900
164 East 68th Street
New York, N.Y. 10021
Contact: Mrs. Judith Porotz, Administrative Coordinator

Auditorium/lecture hall, rehearsal space, conference room, ballroom, exhibit space, classrooms, gymnasium
Seating capacity: 125 in auditorium; 400 in ballroom; 25 in each classroom
Small stage, piano, dance floor, catering facilities; kosher food only may be served

Mosholu-Montefiore Community Center 882-4000
3450 DeKalb Avenue
Bronx, N.Y. 10467
Contact: Freida Leites

Rehearsal space, conference room, exhibit space, lounge
Seating capacity: 150/175

The Museum of Broadcasting 752-4690
1 East 53rd Street
New York, N.Y. 10022
Contact: Ray Liddell, Technical Director

Auditorium
Seating capacity: 63
Complete technical facilities for video-tape projection

New York Academy of Sciences 838-0230
2 East 63rd Street
New York, N.Y. 10021
Contact: Matthew Katz, Meeting Services Director

Auditorium, 4 conference/lecture rooms, ballroom, 18' x 18' planted courtyard, exhibit space, reception area, library
Seating capacity: 20/125
Rental fee: $35 per hour; $250 from 9 a.m. to 5 p.m.
16mm sound motion picture projector, slide projectors, overhead projector, sound system, portable lecturn, kitchen; food may be served (kitchen and banquet staff available)
Space is a townhouse
Suggested uses: banquet, meeting, reception
Note: Space is only available to non-profit groups, particularly those involved in science or medicine, on weekdays

New York Blood Center 570-3184
310 East 67th Street
New York, N.Y. 10021
Contact: James Toner, Administrator

Auditorium, classroom/conference room
Seating capacity: 348 in auditorium; 40 in class/conference room
Rental fee: $250 minimum for auditorium; $150 minimum for 3 hour use of classroom
Stage, piano
Suggested uses: class, lecture, meeting

The New York Geneological & Biographical Society 755-8532
122 East 58th Street
New York, N.Y. 10022
Contact: Mrs. Carolyn G. Stifel, Executive Secretary

Auditorium, meeting room
Seating capacity: 210 in auditorium; 60 in meeting room
Rental fee: $100 donation; $125 if food is served
Platform, sound equipment, kitchen; food may be served
Suggested uses: lecture, meeting
Note: Space is only available to historic, cultural and patriotic groups. Admission charges, fund-raising and sales are not allowed

The Oval Room (212) 466-8169
The Port Authority of New York & New Jersey (201) 622-6600
One World Trade Center ext. 8169
New York, N.Y. 10048
Contact: Roger Marshall, Special Services Representative

Meeting room, reception area, lounge
Seating capacity: 7,000 sq. ft. space consists of an outer reception area encompassing an interior room capable of being transformed into three separate rooms. 30/220 for a single room; 230 auditorium-style/198 for a luncheon/130 classroom-style
Complete audio-visual equipment; food may be served by caterer on premises
Suggested uses: press conference, reception, luncheon, seminar, audio-visual presentation, product display

Phipps Central Harlem Center 749-1157
259 West 123rd Street
New York, N.Y. 10027
Contact: Randy McGee, Director

Auditorium, meeting rooms, gymnasium
Seating capacity: 287 in auditorium
Rental fee: varies with non-profit or profit-making group
Stage, platform, piano, kitchen; food may be served
Suggested uses: dance, etc.

The Queens Museum 592-2405
New York City Building
Flushing Meadow-Corona Park
Flushing, N.Y. 11368
Contact: Janet Katz

Auditorium, large exhibit space, workshop
Seating capacity: 65 in auditorium; 80 in workshop
Rental fee: negotiable
Suggested uses: auction, concert, class, exhibit, meeting, performance, reception

Riverdale-Yonkers Society for Ethical Culture 548-4445
4450 Fieldston Road
Bronx, N.Y. 10471
Contact: Lee Louis, Executive Secretary

Rehearsal space, exhibit space, meeting room, terrace
Seating capacity: 150 in Society Meeting Room

Rental fee: $50 per hour during day; $200 from 8:30 p.m. to 11:00 p.m.
Piano
Suggested uses: auction, concert, class (no desks), exhibit, lecture,
  meeting, performance, promotion, reception, rehearsal

Seamen's Church Institute of New York   269-2710
15 State Street   ext. 322
New York, N.Y. 10004
Contact: Liz Bridster, Hotel, Clubs & Conferences

2 auditoriums, 3 conference rooms, ballroom, exhibit space,
  reception area, cafeteria, dining room, cocktail lounge
Seating capacity: 175 in auditoriums; 250 in ballroom; 25/60 in conference rooms
Rental fee: by contribution
Stage, piano, dance floor, PA system, kitchen; food and beverages
  may be served
Suggested uses: all special events are possible including a banquet or party

Studios 58 Playhouse, Inc.   581-7238
Wellington Hotel — Laurelton Room
55th Street & Seventh Avenue
New York, N.Y. 10019
Contact: Grace Bramson

Rehearsal space/conference room/exhibit space/classroom, reception area
Seating capacity: 250
Steinway B Grand piano, professional lighting, excellent acoustics
Suggested uses: concert, class, exhibit, conference, lecture, reception,
  film, rehearsal, audition

Tibet Center, Inc.   684-8245
114 East 28th Street
New York, N.Y. 10016
Contact: Khyongla Rato

2 conference rooms
Seating capacity: 50/60
Kitchen; food may be served including Tibetan dinners for 25/75
Suggested uses: concert, class, fair, meeting, lecture, reception, wedding

Waterside Swim & Health Club   685-6071
30 Waterside Plaza   685-6148
New York, N.Y. 10010
Contact: Nicholas Stringas

Conference room, patio, swimming pool, exercise room, saunas
Seating capacity: 125 in conference room
Dance floor, kitchen; food may be served
Overlooks the East River
Suggested uses: auction, banquet, class, lecture, meeting,
  party, promotion, reception

William Sobelsohn Associates   575-1500
1540 Broadway (btw. 45th & 46th Streets)
New York, N.Y. 10036
Contact: William Sobelsohn

Classrooms/meeting rooms
Seating capacity: 20/200
Food may be served

Willkie Memorial Building 730-7744
20 West 40th Street
New York, N.Y. 10018
Contact: Leonard Sussman, Executive Director or
  Gertrude Entwistle, Reservations Secretary

Board room, conference room
Seating capacity: 100 in board room; 50 in conference room
Rental fee: $45 for board room; $30 for conference room
Small platform
Suggested uses: class, non-hanging exhibit, lecture, meeting,
  solo performance, reception
Note: Smoking is not allowed. Space is only available during the week
  until 10:30 p.m.

Women's City Club of New York, Inc. 581-2480
6 West 48th Street
New York, N.Y. 10036
Contact: Lorraine Burns, Executive Secretary

Reception area, 2 lounges
Seating capacity: 125 auditorium-style in both lounges
  (May be divided into 20/25 for small lounge, 110/120
  for large lounge)
Rental fee: $100 minimum
Suggested uses: class, lecture, meeting, reception

Workmen's Circle Building 889-6800
45 East 33rd Street
New York, N.Y. 10016
Contact: Jeff Stein

Auditorium, rehearsal space, conference room, ballroom, exhibit space,
  reception area, multi-purpose rooms
Seating capacity: 12/350; 200 banquet style
Rental fee: by regular contract or single function
Platform, piano, dance floor, kitchen; food may be served by caterer
  of your choice
Suggested uses: all special events are possible including a class during the day

Also see: **AUDITORIUMS (Seating 500 or more)**
  CONFERENCE CENTERS
  CHURCHES
  EXHIBIT SPACES
  HOTELS
  LIBRARIES
  LOFTS
  PERFORMANCE SPACES
  SCHOOLS
  Y's

* * * * * * *

Central Park

PARKS & PLAZAS

PARKS

There are approximately 1115 parcels of land under the jurisdiction of the New York City Department of Parks and Recreation. For special events in parks, permits are issued free of charge for cultural and athletic activities. To obtain a special events permit, or to reserve a sporting facility (i.e., baseball field), call the Parks Department Office in the borough which pertains to the location of the event

Manhattan	397-3117
Bronx	822-4566
Brooklyn	965-6523
Queens	520-5331
Staten Island	442-7640

Note: Wedding ceremonies may be held in any park and do not need permits; wedding receptions must be held elsewhere

If you wish to attend a special event that is free call 755-4100 any time of the day or night for a daily tape.

PICNIC AREAS

	Tables	Grill Slabs
Manhattan:		
Fort Washington Park, Riverside Drive & 180th Street	15	0
Ward's Island	50	0
Bronx:		
Crotona Park, Crotona Park East & Charlotte Street	10	0
Pelham Bay Park, Hunter Island, near Orchard Beach	95	0
Pelham Bay Park, Rice Playfield, Bruckner Blvd. at Pelham Bay Station	58	0
Pelham Bay Park, Orchard Beach, south of bus terminal	60	0
Pelham Bay Park, Twin Island, near Orchard Beach	25	0
Van Cortlandt Park, Allen Shandler Recreation Area west of Jerome Ave., at Woodlawn Station	275	0
Van Cortlandt Park, Rockwood Drive, Mosholu Ave., east of Broadway	46	0
Van Cortlandt Park, 233rd Street & Jerome Ave. Allen Shandler Recreation Area	4	0
Brooklyn:		
Manhattan Beach Park, Oriental Blvd., Ocean Ave. to Mackenzie St.	160	48
Prospect Park, near Prospect Park West & Fifth Street	75	0

World Trade Center Plaza

Queens:

Alley Park, Grand Central Parkway & Winchester Blvd., Queens Village	404	90
Alley Park, Springfield Blvd. & 76th Ave., Queens Village	228	46
Brookville Park, Brookville Blvd. & Southern Parkway, Rosedale	75	0
Cunningham Park, south of Union Turnpike & Francis Lewis Blvd.	240	90
Flushing Meadows—Corona Park, Lawrence Street area	28	0
Flushing Meadows—Corona Park, Meadow Lake East area	28	0
Flushing Meadows—Corona Park, Meadow Lake West area	30	0
Forest Park, Main Drive, west of Woodhaven Blvd., Glendale	310	70
Rockaway Beach, Beach 17th Street & Seagirt Blvd.	45	0
Rockaway Beach, Shore Parkway & Beach 87th Street	40	0
Rockaway Beach, Shore Parkway & Beach 99th Street	38	0

Staten Island:

Clove Lakes Park, Clove Road & Victory Blvd.	76	18
South Beach, Fort Wadsworth to Millar Field, Midland Beach	54	0
Willowbrook Park, Richmond Ave. & Victory Blvd.	10	0
Wolfe's Pond Park, Holten & Cornelia Aves., Prince's Bay	6	00

Note: Picknickers need to supply their own grills for use on grill slabs. Grilling, flames, or fires of any sort are not permitted at sites without grill slabs and an adult must be present to supervise the fire.

PLAZAS/MINI-PARKS

Art on the Beach   619-1955
Creative Time, Inc.
66 West Broadway
New York, N.Y. 10007
Contact: Anita O'Neill

Over 10 acres of Battery City landfill can be used by artists whose sculpture and/or performance pieces are both new and specifically designed for the site. Juried entries are performed and/or exhibited during the summer months for as many years as the area remains undeveloped.

Bethune Senior Center   862-6700
1949 Amsterdam Avenue
New York, N.Y. 10032
Contact: Rosie Eugene

Mall
Piano
Rental fee: none
Food may be served
Space is usually available during the summer and during the day in the winter for free performances

Burlington House
1345 Avenue of the Americas
New York, N.Y. 10019
Contact: Anthony Quintano, Executive General Manager,
   Fisher Bros., or Tony Vitrano, Building Manager

752-5000
(Fisher Bros.)
581-7795
(Bldg. Office)

Mini-park
Catered food may be served
Suggested uses: all special events are possible

Chase Manhattan Plaza
1 Chase Manhattan Plaza
New York, N.Y. 10015
Contact: George Jurkowich

552-4407

Large plaza
Rental fee: none
Platform
Suggested uses: concert, performance
Note: Commercial usage and fund-raising are not allowed

88 Pine Street Plaza
88 Pine Street
New York, N.Y. 10005
Contact: Building Management

344-0140

Mini-park

Hammarskjold Plaza Sculpture Garden
866 Second Avenue (at 47th Street)
New York, N.Y. 10017
Contact: Linda or Harry Macklowe

661-0033

Outdoor paved area specifically used for the display of monumental
   sculpture. Concerts, poetry readings and dance performances
   are also possible

Lincoln Center Fountain Plaza

Lincoln Center Plazas
Lincoln Center for the Performing Arts, Inc.
140 West 65th Street
New York, N.Y. 10023
Contact: Leonard de Paur

877-1800

Outdoor plazas with display fountain and reflecting pool
Seating capacity: varies with function
Stage, sound equipment

127 John Street　　　　　　　　　　　　　　　　　　　　　　943-9355
Sage Realty
New York, N.Y. 10038
Contact: Ralph Ardolina or John Silbert

Outdoor area, mini-park
Food may be served through the concession
Suggested uses: party, performance

Roberto Clemente State Park　　　　　　　　　　　　　　　299-8750
(formerly the Harlem River State Park)
(State Park & Recreation Commission for the City of New York)
West Tremont & Matthewson Road
Bronx, N.Y. 10453
Contact: Richard Ortiz, Park Director, or Donald Yerwood,
　　Recreation Supervisor

Rehearsal space, conference room, promenade space, exhibit space,
　　gymnasium with bleachers, swimming pool, playgrounds,
　　basketball court
Seating capacity: 630 in gymnasium
Rental fee: none
Platform, piano; food may be served
Note: Space is only available for use with a permit

77 Water Street　　　　　　　　　　　　　　　　　　　　　　422-7277
Sage Realty Corporation
New York, N.Y. 10005
Contact: Ralph Ardolina, Building Manager

Outdoor area, mini-park
Food may be served through the concession
Suggested uses: exhibit, party

World Trade Center Plaza　　　　　　　　　　　　　　　　　466-4233
The Port Authority of New York and New Jersey
One World Trade Center
New York, N.Y. 10048
Contact: Marie Putignano, Public Services Coordinator

World Trade Center Plaza comprises 5 acres of outdoor space.
　　Suitable for performances, fairs, display of sizeable equipment

Also see: Brooklyn Botanic Garden
　　　　　ENVIRONMENTAL CENTERS
　　　　　New York Botanical Garden
　　　　　Queens Botanical Garden

* * * * * * *

For **PENTHOUSES, TERRACES & VIEWS** see: **HOTELS**
　　　　　　　　　　　　　　　　　　　　　　LOFTS
　　　　　　　　　　　　　　　　　　　　　　PRIVATE PARTIES/PRIVATE PLACES
　　　　　　　　　　　　　　　　　　　　　　PRIVATE PARTIES/PUBLIC PLACES

PERFORMANCE SPACES

(CONCERT/RECITAL)

Abraham Goodman House   362-8060
Home of the Hebrew Arts School
129 West 67th Street
New York, N.Y. 10023
Contact: Lydia Kontos or Jessie Berger

Concert hall, recital hall, exhibit hall, music library, music practice studios, 2 dance studios
Seating capacity: 457 in concert hall; 130 in recital hall
35' x 26' concert stage, platform, piano, dance floor, dressing rooms
Suggested uses: concert, rehearsal, recording, audition
Note: Space is not available on Friday evenings or Saturday during the day

Alice Tully Hall   580-8700
Lincoln Center for the Performing Arts, Inc.
65th Street & Broadway
New York, N.Y. 10023
Contact: Delmar Hendricks, Booking Manager

Auditorium
Seating capacity: 1096
Rental fee: $1,200 plus labor during the evening
21'6" x 50' stage, piano, motion picture projector, sound equipment; catered food only may be served

Avery Fisher Hall   580-8700
Lincoln Center for the Performing Arts, Inc.
Lincoln Center Plaza
65th Street & Broadway
New York, N.Y. 10023
Contact: Delmar Hendricks, Booking Manager

Auditorium
Seating capacity: 2738
Rental fee: varies from $725 to $3,000 per performance; $175 for 2½/3 hour rehearsal period. Fees exclude labor charges
40'4" x 68' stage, piano, motion picture projector; food may be served only by space's own caterer

Bardavon 1869 Opera House   (914) 473-2072
35 Market Street
Poughkeepsie, N.Y. 12601
Contact: Teresa Manzi

75 miles north of New York City, this restored Opera House is the seventh oldest in the country and the oldest in New York State.

"Concert" Lincoln Center

Seating capacity: 900
Available to groups for benefit performances of a Broadway
    show, opera, dance, philharmonic concert, chamber music
    and children's theatre
Art exhibit area in outer lobby

Bloomingdale House of Music   663-6021
323 West 108th Street
New York, N.Y. 10025
Contact: David Greer

Auditorium, limited rehearsal space, exhibit space, lounge,
    reception room, classrooms, library, small garden
Seating capacity: 70 in auditorium
Rental fee: negotiable
Space is a townhouse

Brooklyn Academy of Music   636-4144
30 Lafayette Avenue
Brooklyn, N.Y. 11217
Contact: Leonard Natman or John Miller

Opera house, playhouse, flexible space
Seating capacity: 2100 in opera house; 1100 in Helen Carey Playhouse;
    500 bleacher style seating in 5250 sq. ft. Leperq Space
2 stages, platform, piano, performance area, motion picture projector,
    sound equipment, theatrical lighting

Brooklyn College   780-5296
Bedford Avenue & Avenue H
Brooklyn, N.Y. 11210
Contact: Richard Grossberg

2 auditoriums
Seating capacity: 2488 in Whitman Hall (professional concert hall);
    504 in Gershwin Hall
Rental fee: $2,300 for Whitman Hall; $1,000 for 5 hours in Gershwin Hall
Stage, platform, piano, 35mm motion picture projector, sound equipment,
    concert lighting, video taping and filming, light refreshments
    may be served

Calderone Concert Hall   (516) 747-4320
145 North Franklin Street
Hempstead, N.Y. 11550
Contact: Carol Strutt or Helen Neushaefer

Auditorium, rehearsal space, classroom, conference room,
    exhibit space, reception area
Seating capacity: 2400
Rental fee: depends on event
Stage, platform, 35mm motion picture projector, kitchen;
    food may be served
Suggested uses: auction, concert, class, exhibit, lecture,
    meeting, party, performance, promotion, reception

Cami Hall   397-6981
(formerly Judson Hall)
165 West 57th Street
New York, N.Y. 10019
Contact: Richard E. Hansen, Manager

Concert hall
Seating capacity: 240
Rental fee: varies with day and time from $120 to $255;
  hourly rates vary from $24 to $36. Additional charge for
  other services and equipment
Stage, platform, concert grand pianos, concert lighting
Suggested uses: auction, concert, class, exhibit, lecture, meeting,
  rehearsal, performance, promotion, audition

The Carnegie Hall Corporation 397-8763
Carnegie Recital Hall
154 West 57th Street
New York, N.Y. 10019
Contact: Gilda Barlas Weissberger, Booking Manager

Main Hall, auditorium, rehearsal space
Seating capacity: 2800 in Main Hall; 297 in auditorium
40' x 60' x 43' stage, piano, organ and sound equipment
  in Main Hall; 33' x 21' stage and piano in auditorium
Suggested uses: concert, lecture, meeting, performance

Five Towns Music and Art Foundation (516) 569-0011
Broadway & Johnson Place
Woodmere, N.Y. 11598
Contact: Louise Kaminow, Auditorium Coordinator

Auditorium, conference/music room
Seating capacity: 160/200 in auditorium; 40/60 in conference room
Rental fee: $25 to $35 weekday during the day/$30 to $45 weekday
  during the evening/$120 weekend during the day/$45 to $90 during
  the evening for the auditorium; $25 for the conference room.
  Space may be rented once a week or once a month for regular use.
  Additional fee for custodian during the weekend
Stage, piano, dance floor; refreshments may be served
Suggested uses: all special events are possible except a banquet,
  professional dance, fair, promotion, reception or wedding

Greenwich House Music School 242-4770
46 Barrow Street
New York, N.Y. 10014
Contact: John S. Winkleman, Director

Auditorium, rehearsal space, classroom, exhibit space, courtyard/garden
Seating capacity: 80 in Renee Weiler Concert Hall; 30 in classroom
Rental fee: $175 for auditorium and courtyard; varies per hour
  for rehearsal space and classroom
Stage, 2 pianos, harpsichord
Music oriented groups are particularly welcome
Suggested uses: concert, class, exhibit, lecture, meeting, performance,
  reception

The Solomon R. Guggenheim Museum 860-1365
1071 Fifth Avenue (btw. 89th & 90th Streets)
New York, N.Y. 10028
Contact: Vanessa Jalet

Auditorium
Seating capacity: 299
Stage, 16mm film projector, slide projector, sound equipment
Suggested uses: concert, lecture, dance performance
Note: Space has limited availability

John Andrew Spaulding's Jazz Gallery　　　　　　　　　　　　　　　875-0853
55 West 19th Street
New York, N.Y. 10011
Contact: Ms. Cobi Narita

Performance space
Seating capacity: 100 sitdown
Rental fee: approximately $450
Stage, upright piano, professional sound equipment, bar;
　food may be served
Suggested uses: concert, meeting, performance, workshop, party

Lehman College Center for the Performing Arts　　　　　　　　　860-8232
Bedford Park Boulevard West
Bronx, N.Y. 10468
Contact: Alan Light, Managing Director, or
　Valerie Simmons, Assistant Director

Concert Hall
Seating capacity: 2310

Library and Museum of the Performing Arts　　　　　　　　　　　870-1613
111 Amsterdam Avenue　　　　　　　　　　　　　　　　　　　　　　930-0800
New York, N.Y. 10023　　　　　　　　　　　　　　　　　　　　　　(switchboard)
Contact: Joan Canale

Auditorium, conference room, exhibit space
Seating capacity: 212
Rental fee: none if event is open to the public
Stage, piano, motion picture projectors, sound equipment;
　food may be served

Manhattan School of Music　　　　　　　　　　　　　　　　　　　749-2802
120 Claremont Avenue
New York, N.Y. 10027
Contact: Jack Sproule

Auditorium/rehearsal space, recital hall
Seating capacity: 988 in John Borden Auditorium; 325 in recital hall
Rental fee: varies
Stage, platform, piano
Suggested uses: concert, lecture, recital

Metropolitan Opera Association, Inc.　　　　　　　　　　　　　　799-3100
Lincoln Center for the Performing Arts, Inc.
Lincoln Center Plaza
Broadway & 63rd Street
New York, N.Y. 10023
Contact: Presentations Department

Auditorium
Seating capacity: 4000
54' x 54' proscenium stage; catered food may be served

Queens College　　　　　　　　　　　　　　　　　　　　　　　　520-7200
Long Island Expressway & Kissena Boulevard
Flushing, N.Y. 11367
Contact: Lawrence Ferrar, Campus Facilities Officer

Rathaus Recital Hall
Seating capacity: 220

Radio City Music Hall (212) 246-0945
1260 Avenue of the Americas
New York, N.Y. 10020
Contact: Sales Department

Auditorium, rehearsal space, exhibit space, reception area
Seating capacity: 5,882 in auditorium
Rental fee: upon request
Proscenium stage, piano, motion picture projector & screen,
    Dolby sound system, stage elevators & turntable, food services,
    organ, production staff
Suggested uses: all special events are possible including a concert,
    lecture, performance or convention

Symphony Space, Inc. 865-2557
2537 Broadway (at 95th Street)
New York, N.Y. 10025
Contact: Allan Miller, Artistic Director, Isaiah Sheffer,
    Artistic Director or Linda Rogers, Managing Director

Auditorium, rehearsal space
Seating capacity: 922
Rental fee: varies; none if performance is free
Stage, platform, piano
Space is a non-profit community performing arts center
Suggested uses: concert, lecture, dance

Third Street Music School Settlement 777-3240
235 East 11th Street
New York, N.Y. 10003
Contact: Frederick Wise or MaryLou Francis

Auditorium/amphitheatre, rehearsal space, recital room,
    reception area, dance studio
Seating capacity: 325 in approximately 40' x 80' auditorium;
    70 in recital room
Auditorium has tiered seating surrounding an oval wood floor,
    upright and grand pianos
Suggested uses: concert, class, lecture, meeting, performance,
    music and dance recital

Town Hall 997-1003
123 West 43rd Street
New York, N.Y. 10036
Contact: Mr. Zucker

Concert hall
Seating capacity: 1498
Suggested uses: concert, lecture, recital
Space is a 60-year-old landmark

Turtle Bay Music School 753-8811
244 East 52nd Street
New York, N.Y. 10022
Contact: Janet M. Robbins, Executive Director

Auditorium
Seating capacity: 175
Rental fee: varies with function
Stage, piano, sound equipment, stationary spot lights
Suggested uses: meeting, recital, play

Also see: Association of Artist-Run Galleries
BANDSHELLS
Bargemusic, Ltd.
LIBRARIES
LOFTS
PARKS & PLAZAS
PERFORMANCE SPACES (Dance/Theatre)
PIERS
SCHOOLS & COLLEGES

BANDSHELLS

Manhattan:

Central Park Mall
72nd Street, center of park — 397-3116 for permit

Colonial Park
Bradhurst Avenue and West 147th Street

Damrosch Park, Guggenheim Bandshell
West 62nd Street and Amsterdam Avenue

East River Park
East River Drive, below Grand Street

Marcus Garvey Park, Richard Rodgers Bandshell
Mount Morris Park West and 122nd Street

Tompkins Square Park
East 7th Street and Avenue A

Bronx:

Franz Siegel Park
Grand Concourse & East 153rd Street — 822-4236 for permit

Haffen Park
Gunther, Ely & Hammersley Avenues

Poe Park
East 192nd Street & Grand Concourse

Brooklyn:

Prospect Park
11th Street Playground, off West Drive and
Prospect Park West at 11th Street — 965-6523 for permit

Prospect Park Music Grove
West of East Drive and south of Center Drive

Seaside Park
Seabreeze & Surf Avenues

Queens:

Forest Park
Main Drive, west of Woodhaven Boulevard, Glendale — 520-5331 for permit

* * * * *

PERFORMANCE SPACES

(DANCE/THEATER)

Actor's Playhouse   741-1215
100 Seventh Avenue South
New York, N.Y. 10014
Contact: Jack Ross or Charles Timm, Producers

Auditorium, rehearsal space
Seating capacity: 150
Rental fee: $250 for Saturday afternoon or during the evening on Monday
Proscenium stage, piano; food may be served
Suggested uses: auction, concert, class, social or professional dance, exhibit, lecture, meeting, party, performance, promotion

    316 East 91st Street
    New York, N.Y. 10028

    Theatre
    Seating capacity: 299
    Rental fee: $350 after 10:30 p.m. or during the evening on Monday
    Large stage, piano

Actors Repertory Theatre   687-6430
Warren Robertson Theatre Workshop
303 East 44th Street
New York, N.Y. 10017
Contact: Toon Astenberg

Auditorium, rehearsal space, classroom, conference room
Seating capacity: 90/100
Rental fee: $100 per evening
Stage, piano
Suggested uses: auction, concert, class, exhibit, lecture, meeting, party, performance, promotion, reception, wedding

The American Mime Theatre   777-1710
24 Bond Street
New York, N.Y. 10012
Contact: Paul J. Curtis, Director or Jean Barbour, Administrator

Upstairs studio/rehearsal space, downstairs meeting room/classroom/studio
Seating capacity: 50 in upstairs studio, 30 in downstairs meeting room
Inner stage, kitchen; food may be served
Suggested uses: class, lecture, meeting, reception

City Center/55th Street Dance Theater Foundation, Inc.

American Place Theatre
111 West 46th Street
New York, N.Y. 10036
Contact: Joanna Vedder, General Manager

246-3730

Theatre/auditorium, experimental theatre/classroom/conference room, cabaret/reception area
Seating capacity: 350 in theatre, 75 in experimental theatre, 75 in cabaret
Rental fee: upon request
Proscenium stage, platform, piano, complete lighting and sound equipment, bar; food may be served
Suggested uses: all special events are possible, including a fashion show, sales meeting or audition, except for a banquet, class, social dance, fair, party or wedding

American Theatre of Actors
314 West 54th Street
New York, N.Y. 10019
Contact: James Jennings

581-3044

3 indoor performance spaces, 1 outdoor performance space
Seating capacity: 99, 70, 41 for indoor performance spaces
Rental fee: $185 per performance for 99 seat space; $85 per performance for 70 seat space; $55 per performance for 41 seat space: $100 per performance for outdoor space
Proscenium or three-quarter stages, professional sound and lighting equipment, dimmer board
Suggested use: performance

Association of Artist-Run Galleries, Inc.
152 Wooster Street
New York, N.Y. 10012
Contact: Marilyn Belford, Director

533-0354

Informal theatre in the round, exhibit space
Seating capacity: approximately 200 people may be accommodated in 2,000 sq. ft. open space (may be subdivided into 1,000 sq. ft. space)
Rental fee: $150 per event
Suggested uses: art-related auction, concert, exhibit, lecture, meeting, performance, video, film, poetry reading, etc.
Note: Cultural events only are allowed. Space owns 22 galleries with similar spaces at varying rental fees. Sponsorship of music composers and poets

Beacon Theatre
2124 Broadway (at 74th Street)
New York, N.Y. 10023
Contact: Janice Ginsberg

737-7536

Auditorium, theatre, rehearsal space, conference room, exhibit space, dance rehearsal area
Seating capacity: 1328 orchestra; 542 loge; 283 lower balcony; 492 upper balcony in auditorium
Rental fee: negotiable
Stage, platform, piano, dance floor, motion picture projector, sound equipment, rising orchestra pit, lights; complete theatrical stage facilities
Fully equipped landmark theatre with a 1920's decor
Suggested uses: all special events are possible, including an opera and videotaping, except for a banquet, fair or wedding

Bouwerie Lane Theatre 677-0060
330 Bowery
New York, N.Y. 10012
Contact: Andy Cohn

Auditorium/theatre, rehearsal space, reception area
Seating capacity: 140 in auditorium
Stage
Suggested uses: auction, concert, class, lecture, meeting, party, performance, film location

Caranci Studios 924-5295
22 West 15th Street
New York, N.Y. 10011
Contact: John Caranci

5 studios
Seating capacity: 50 in 54' x 24' studio; 42' x 24', 32' x 18', 15' x 16' and 15' x 15' of space is available in the other studios
Rental fee: negotiable
Suitable for dancers and actors. New dance floors
Suggested uses: rehearsal, musical comedy

Carter Theatre 391-1880
250 West 43rd Street
New York, N.Y. 10036
Contact: Jim Payne, General Manager

Auditorium, rehearsal space, reception area
Seating capacity: 199
Rental fee: $1,200 per week; $200 per performance; $20 per hour for rehearsal or non-performance
Proscenium stage, piano
Suggested uses: auction, concert, class, professional dance, lecture, meeting, performance

Charas/New Assembly Performance Space 982-0627
605 East 9th Street
New York, N.Y. 10009
Contact: Emily Rubin or Chino Garcia

Theatre, terrace room/theatre, classroom, gymnasium
Seating capacity: 390 in theatre; 100 in 28' x 45' terrace room; 21' x 21' of space available in classroom; 25' x 45' of space available in hardwood floor gymnasium
Rental fee: $5.00 per hour (excluding lighting equipment) day or evening; extended use negotiable
Proscenium stage, upright piano, sound and lighting equipment, kitchen; food may be served; 12' ceilings minimum
Suggested uses: class, social or professional dance, meeting, performance, benefit

Circle in The Square (Uptown) 581-3270
1633 Broadway (at 50th Street)
New York, N.Y. 10019
Contact: Theodore Mann, Artistic Director and Owner

Theatre in the round, rehearsal space
Seating capacity: 680

Circle In The Square (Downtown)
159 Bleecker Street
New York, N.Y. 10012

Theatre in the round, rehearsal space
Seating capacity: 299

City Center 55th Street Theater   247-0430
131 West 55th Street
New York, N.Y. 10019
Contact: Ting Barrow, Associate Director

Auditorium, rehearsal space, exhibit space
Seating capacity: 2932 in 55th Street Theater; 499 in Downstairs Theater
Stage, platform, piano, dance floor
Suggested uses: auction, concert, class, exhibit, fair, lecture, meeting, performance, promotion

Colonnades Theatre Lab, Inc.   598-4620
428 Lafayette Street
New York, N.Y. 10003
Contact: Robin Rose

Auditorium, theatre in the round, rehearsal space, exhibit space, reception area
Seating capacity: 120 in theatre (raked seating)
Rental fee: $1,000 to $1,200 per week (fully equipped); $8 to $10 per hour
Stage, piano, fireplace, winding staircase, kitchen; food may be served
Suggested uses: all special events are possible except a concert or fair

Dance Theater Workshop, Inc.   691-6500
American Theatre Laboratory
219 West 19th Street (2nd floor)
New York, N.Y. 10011
Contact: David White, Executive Director; Robert Applegarth, Associate Director for Programs or Phil Sandstrom, Production Manager

Black box theater, dance studio, classroom
Seating capacity: 100 in theater; 31' x 35' of space available in studio
32' x 26' performing area (with wings in place), pianos, dance floor, theatrical lighting, sound equipment, wood floor (in studio)
Performance space books fairly far in advance. Applications after Jan. 1st are applied to performance year July through June. Some class and rehearsal space available on shorter notice.
Suggested uses: rehearsal, presentation of dance, dance related artists, theater and music events

Dramatis Personae   468-8285
25 East 4th Street
New York, N.Y. 10003
Contact: Steven Baker, President

Rehearsal space, classroom, conference room, exhibit space
Seating capacity: 150
Rental fee: negotiable
Proscenium stage, platform, dance floor; food may be served by caterer of your choice
Suggested uses: all special events are possible including club meetings, except for a banquet, fair, party, reception or wedding

Dennis Wayne's Dancerschool Ltd. 737-7536
400 Lafayette Street
New York, N.Y. 10003

Rehearsal space, exhibit space, reception area, 5 studios
Seating capacity: 17,000 sq. ft. of space is available;
   15,000 sq. ft. of studio space
Piano, dance floor; food may be served by caterer of your choice
Rental fee: negotiable, depending upon day, time and duration
So-Ho loft environment
Suggested uses: auction, banquet, concert, class, exhibit, lecture,
   meeting, party, promotion, reception, wedding

Donnell Library Center 621-0613
20 West 53rd Street
New York, N.Y. 10019
Contact: Philip Gerrard

Auditorium, exhibit space
Seating capacity: 278
Rental fee: varies from $60 to $160
Stage, piano, motion picture projector, sound equipment

Edison Theater 586-7870
240 West 47th Street
New York, N.Y. 10036
Contact: Norman Kean

Auditorium, rehearsal space, lounge, dressing rooms
Seating capacity: 500
Stage, piano, motion picture projector; food may be served
Suggested uses: lecture, sales meeting, fashion show, industrial conference

Entermedia Theater 777-6230
189 Second Avenue (at 12th Street)
New York, N.Y. 10003
Contact: Joseph Asaro

Auditorium/theater, rehearsal space, conference room, reception area,
   lounge, cafe
Seating capacity: 1077 in auditorium; 25' x 40' of rehearsal space is available
Rental fee: negotiable
Stage, proscenium stage, kitchen; food may be served at the cafe;
   catering available
Suggested uses: all special events are possible including video-taping a
   live show, filming, TV commercial, except a banquet, exhibit or fair

42nd Street Theatre Row, Inc. 279-8822
330 West 42nd Street (26th floor)
New York, N.Y. 10036
Contact: Barbara Grove, Development Director

Auditoriums, rehearsal space, classrooms, dance studios
Composed of ten member theatrical groups, housed in 7 buildings
   containing 9 performance spaces and 20 floors of rehearsal and
   office space. 120 sq. ft. is the maximum available in each theatre;
   seating for approximately 100
Rental fee: varies with space and function
Proscenium stages, platforms, pianos, dance floors; food may be served
   by caterer of your choice or by space
Suggested uses: concert, class, professional dance, lecture, performance,
   rehearsal, etc.

Foundation for the Advance of Dance 989-2250
55 Bethune Street (630A)
New York, N.Y. 10014
Contact: E. Kapel

Rehearsal space
Seating capacity: 25/50
Dance floor, mirrors, barres
Overlooks the Hudson River
Suggested uses: rehearsal, small performance, class

Gene Frankl Theatre Workshop, Inc. 581-2775
36 West 62nd Street
New York, N.Y. 10023
Contact: Ann Katcher

Theatre space, rehearsal space
Seating capacity: 80 in theatre space
Stage
Suggested uses: concert (no rock), lecture, meeting, party, performance

Gramercy Arts Theater 889-2850
138 East 27th Street
New York, N.Y. 10016
Contact: Robert Federico

Auditorium
Seating capacity: 180
Proscenium stage, piano
Suggested uses: auction, concert, class, lecture, meeting, performance

Guild Rehearsal Studios 874-1279
2109 Broadway (at 73rd Street)
New York, N.Y. 10023
Contact: M. Bozza

5 rehearsal studios, theater
Seating capacity: 30 x 20 to 50 x 25 sq. ft. of space available
  in rehearsal studio; 75/90 in theater
Rental fee: varies
Stage, platform, piano, dance floor, sound equipment, theatrical lighting
Suggested uses: dance, theater, recital or voice rehearsal

Harlequin Rehearsal Studio 582-0120
203 West 46th Street
New York, N.Y. 10036
Contact: Desk Manager

10 rehearsal rooms, conference rooms
Seating capacity: 100
Platform, pianos, dance floor; food may be served by caterer
  of your choice
Suggested uses: all special events are possible except a banquet,
  reception or wedding

Hunter College Concert Bureau 570-5410
695 Park Avenue (btw. 67th & 68th Streets)
New York, N.Y. 10021
Contact: Renting Director

Assembly hall, playhouse
Seating capacity: 2185 in assembly hall; 692 in playhouse

Rental fee: $1,300 for assembly hall; $900 for playhouse
  for 5 hours. Additional charge for equipment
Stage, piano, motion picture projector, sound equipment
Suggested uses: concert, lecture, meeting, performance
Note: Space is only available to non-profit groups

Irish Arts Center 757-3318
553 West 51st Street
New York, N.Y. 10019
Contact: Nye Heron

Rehearsal space
Seating capacity: 85
Stage, platform, dance floor
Note: Space is only available Monday through Friday during the day

Jacob Riis Houses Amphitheater 777-8756
454 East Tenth Street 228-2400
New York, N.Y. 10009
Contact: Mrs. Brezovsky

Amphitheater
Seating capacity: 800 plus 100/500 standees
Rental fee: none
Note: Space is only available to non-profit community groups,
  not of a religious or political nature, especially during the summer

James Weldon Johnson Community Centers, Inc. 860-7261
2205 First Avenue (at 114th Street)
New York, N.Y. 10029
Contact: James Robinson, Director

Auditorium, outdoor theater, exhibit space
Seating capacity: 300 in auditorium; 500 in outdoor theater
Stage, platform, dance floor; food may be served by caterer
  of your choice
Suggested uses: all special events are possible except a promotion

Know How Workshop 741-1205
17 West 17th Street
New York, N.Y. 10011
Contact: Greg Alland, Administrator

Rehearsal space, classrooms
Seating capacity: 15/20 in each classroom
Rental fee: $20 per hour
Suggested uses: class, lecture, promotion

Light Opera of Manhattan 861-2287
334 East 74th Street
New York, N.Y. 10021
Contact: Barbara Marsh, Acting Conference Manager

Auditorium
Seating capacity: 274
Stage, backstage dressing rooms
Suggested uses: auction, concert, class, exhibit, lecture, meeting,
  performance, promotion
Note: Space is only available on Mondays

Manhattan Punch Line Theatre   921-8288
260 West 41st Street (7th floor)
New York, N.Y. 10036
Contact: Mitch McGuire or Steve Kaplan

Auditorium, rehearsal space, exhibit space, reception area
Seating capacity: 105 in theatre; 150 in reception area
Rental fee: $150 per evening; $550 to $750 per week;
    $2000 to $3000 per month
Stage, piano
Suggested uses: all special events are possible except a banquet or fair

Manhattan Theater Club   288-2500
321 East 73rd Street
New York, N.Y. 10021
Contact: Paul Fitzmorris

3 auditoriums, 3 rehearsal rooms, cabaret
Seating capacity: 100/150 in auditoriums; 30' x 35'; 22' x 28', and
    40' x 40' of space is available in each rehearsal room
Pianos, 2 dance floors, intercom
Suggested uses: class, lecture, meeting, rehearsal, audition, dance
Note: Performance space is only available during the summer

Merce Cunningham Studio   691-9751
463 West Street
New York, N.Y. 10014
Contact: Michael Bloom, Administrator

Rehearsal space, concert/dance performance space
Seating capacity: 150
Rental fee: $125 per performance; hourly rates are available
Piano, dance floor
Suggested uses: concert, dance class, social or professional dance,
    performance

Morse Mime Theatre   242-0530
224 Waverly Place
New York, N.Y. 10014
Contact: Ellen M. Pollan, Administrator or
    Richard Morse, Director

Rehearsal space, classroom, exhibit space
Seating capacity: 109 maximum
Rental fee: $15 per hour for rehearsal; negotiable rate for other uses
Stage, piano
Suggested uses: class, exhibit, lecture, meeting, performance

The Nameless Theatre   242-9768
125 West 22nd Street   929-4480
New York, N.Y. 10011
Contact: Patrick J. Byrne, Director

Rehearsal space, backyard
Seating capacity: 79
Rental fee: $100 per day; weekly rates are available
Proscenium stage, platform, piano
Suggested uses: all special events are possible except a banquet,
    dance, promotion, reception or wedding

Nat Horne Theatre   736-7128
140 West 42nd Street
New York, N.Y. 10036
Contact: Al Reyes, Artistic Director

Theatre, 2 rehearsal spaces, classroom
Seating capacity: 115 in theatre, 23' x 40' in each rehearsal space
Rental fee: $1,000 per week inclusive of equipment for theatre;
    $15 per hour for rehearsal space with mirrors and dance floor
Proscenium stage, piano, dance floor
Suggested uses: small concert, dance class, lecture, meeting,
    performance

New Dramatists, Inc.   757-6960
424 West 44th Street
New York, N.Y. 10036
Contact: Joy Blacksmith, Projects Director

Auditorium, rehearsal space, small conference room, studio
Seating capacity: 100 in auditorium
Rental fee: negotiable
Stage, flexible platform, sound system, theatrical lighting, kitchen;
    food may be served
Suggested uses: lecture, meeting
Note: Space has limited avialability especially from October to April

New York City Mission Society, Mission Town House   368-8400
646 Lenox Avenue
New York, N.Y. 10037
Contact: Marilyn Nance

Auditorium, theater space
Seating capacity: 716 auditorium-style/500 for a dance in auditorium;
    150 in theatre space
Rental fee: $650 for 6 hours in auditorium; $300 and up for a
    3 to 4 hour meeting in auditorium or theater
Platform, piano, motion picture projector, kitchen (minimum charge);
    food may be served
Suggested uses: concert, dance, meeting
Note: Space is available Friday and Saturday evenings; Sunday day
    and evening

Newfoundland   255-4991
6 West 18th Street
New York, N.Y. 10011
Contact: James Barbosa or Chris Brandt

Theatre space, rehearsal space
Seating capacity: 74; theatre has flexible seating
Rental fee: $125 to $150 per performance, negotiable depending
    on number of performances and performers involved; hourly
    rentals available
Stage, platform, piano, dance floor; food may be served on occasion
Suggested uses: concert, class, professional dance, meeting,
    theatre performance

No Smoking Playhouse   582-7862
354 West 45th Street
New York, N.Y. 10036
Contact: Norman Marshall

Auditorium
Seating capacity: 70
Rental fee: $700 per week or $100 per day
Proscenium stage
Suggested uses: auction, concert, class, lecture, meeting, performance

Nola Sound Studios, Inc.   582-1417
1780 Broadway
New York, N.Y. 10019
Contact: Mildred Rosenbaum

5 rehearsal spaces
Seating capacity: 125/150
Steinway Grand piano in each space
Suggested uses: class, lecture, meeting, piano instruction and practice,
    singing, play rehearsal, fashion show, television show

Off Center Theatre   929-8299
436 West 18th Street
New York, N.Y. 10011
Contact: Daniel Thomas Field

Theatre, rehearsal space, reception area
Seating capacity: 100
Rental fee: $150 per evening (extra charge for kitchen)
Proscenium stage, platform, piano, dance floor, kitchen;
    food may be served by caterer of your choice
Suggested uses: All special events are possible except an exhibit,
    fair, meeting, promotion, reception or wedding

One Astor Plaza   575-0725
1515 Broadway
New York, N.Y. 10036
Contact: Minskoff Rehearsal Studios

11 studios/rehearsal spaces
Seating capacity: 25 seated in larger studios
Pianos, floor to ceiling mirrors;
Suggested uses: meeting, party, reception, rehearsal, audition

The Open Eye   534-6363
316 East 88th Street
New York, N.Y. 10028
Contact: Bonnie Keyes, Administrative Assistant

2 theatrical performing spaces, garden
33' x 33' x 14.5': Lower Space; 72' x 30': Upper Space
Seating capacity: 135 in Lower Space; 160 in Upper Space
Lower Space has a proscenium with a stage floor 3' above
    the main playing area. Sound and lighting equipment.
    Dance and other performing styles
Upper Space is formed by a gabled roof of steel beams 45'
    overhead. Dressing rooms, minimal lighting equipment.
    Environmental feeling invites imaginative staging
Building is located within a church complex
Suggested uses: dance, theater, music performance

The Palladium   249-7773
126 East 14th Street
New York, N.Y. 10003
Contact: Peter Kapp, Ron Delsener Enterprises

Theatre, rehearsal space
Seating capacity: 3387 in theatre
Proscenium stage; concession stand
Suggested uses: all special events are possible including a concert
   or a closed circuit telecast
Note: Call for other theatres which are available for rent for special events

The Production Company 691-7359
249 West 18th Street
New York, N.Y. 10011
Contact: Norman Rene, Artistic Director or
   Caren Harder, Managing Director

Rehearsal/performance space
Seating capacity: 65
Rental fee: negotiable per week; $85 per performance;
   $7.50 per hour
Flexible stage, piano
Suggested uses: class, performance

Richard Allen Center for Culture & Art 496-0120
36 West 62nd Street (4th floor)
New York, N.Y. 10023
Contact: Shirley Radcliff or Toney Blue

Theatre (semi-round)/rehearsal space, exhibit space
Seating capacity: 100 in theatre; approximately 75/100
   in exhibit space
Rental fee: negotiable
Oak platform; refreshments may be served
Suggested uses: concert, class, exhibit, lecture, meeting,
   performance, reception

Larry Richardson's Dance Gallery 685-5972
242 East 14th Street
New York, N.Y. 10003
Contact: J. Anthony Siciliano, Manager

Performance space/gymnasium
Seating capacity: 260 in 50' x 70' x 20' space
Rental fee: $85 during evening
Proscenium stage or in the round, piano, theatrical lighting,
   sound equipment, dressing rooms, velours (can be made into
   a black box); food may be served

78th Street Theatre Lab 595-0850
American Lyric Theatre Workshop
236 West 78th Street
New York, N.Y. 10024
Contact: Mark Zeller, Director

Theatre in the round (2 sides)
Seating capacity: 74
Rental fee; $25 per hour during the day; $150 minimum during the evening
Stage, platform, piano, dance floor
Suggested uses: auction, concert, class, lecture, meeting, performance

SoHo Repertory Theatre 925-2588
19 Mercer Street
New York, N.Y. 10013
Contact: Marlene Swartz, Co-Artistic Director

Three-sided theatre
Seating capacity: 95
Rental fee: negotiable
Unraised stage, piano
Space is a reconverted fabric warehouse
Suggested uses: auction, concert, class, lecture, meeting

Spanish Theater Repertory Company, Ltd. 889-2850
138 East 27th Street
New York, N.Y. 10016
Contact: Gilberto Zaldivar, Producer

Auditorium
Seating capacity: 160
Rental fee: $250
Stage, piano, spot lights, dimmer boards, tape deck

Thalia Spanish Theatre 729-3880
41-17 Greenpoint Avenue
Sunnyside, N.Y. 11104
Contact: Sylvia Brito

Theatre space, lobby
Seating capacity: 100
Stage, platforms, semi-professional sound equipment, dimmer
    boards, dressing rooms; refreshments may be served
Suggested uses: concert, class, meeting, performance, rehearsal
Note: Space is only available on Mondays and Thursdays or
    on weekends when between productions

Theater De Lys 924-2817
121 Christopher Street
New York, N.Y. 10014
Contact: Ben Sprecher, General Manager

Auditorium
Seating capacity: 299
22' x 24' thrust stage, electronic dimmer boards
Suggested uses: concert, lecture, performance, promotion

Theatre, Opera, Music Institute, Inc. 787-3980
(Tomi, Inc.)
23 West 73rd Street (16th floor)
New York, N.Y. 10023
Contact: Jonathan Silver, General Manager

Theatre/meeting/classroom, reception area, terraces
Seating capacity: approximately 75/150; 25' x 40' theatre
Rental fee: varies from $15 to $40 per hour; weekly rates are available
Thrust stage, platform, 4 pianos, theatrical lighting, dressing rooms
Panoramic view of New York City
Suggested uses: all special events are possible except an auction,
    exhibit, fair, or wedding

Theatre 22 243-2805
54 West 22nd Street
New York, N.Y. 10010
Contact: Sidney Armus, Owner

Theatre, rehearsal space, classroom
Seating capacity: 72 in 30' x 20' theatre; 20' x 20' classroom
Rental fee: $35 per performance in theatre; $5.00 to $6.00 per hour
  for rehearsal space
Stage, platform, piano, dance floor, dressing room, kitchen;
  food may be served
Space is a loft
Suggested uses: concert, class, social or professional dance, lecture,
  meeting, party, performance

Thirteenth Street Theatre 675-6677
50 West 13th Street
New York, N.Y. 10011
Contact: Edith O'Hara

Theatre, rehearsal space, lobby
Seating capacity: 75 in theatre; 15' x 25' of rehearsal space is available;
  30 in lobby
Rental fee: $100 per evening for theatre; $6.00 per hour for stage
  ($10.00 per hour with lights); $5.00 per hour for rehearsal space
Stage, platform, piano, kitchen; food may be served
Suggested uses: all special events are possible including a children's
  birthday party service, except a dance, fair or wedding

Union Square Theatre 598-4430
Theatrium
5 East 16th Street (10th floor)
New York, N.Y. 10003
Contact: Lee Pucklis, Associate Director and Rental Agent

Rehearsal space, classroom, exhibit space
Seating capacity: 125; 4500 sq. ft. of space is available
Rental fee: negotiable
Platforms, piano, roll-up Marley dance floor, dressing rooms,
  mirrored wall, theatrical lighting; food may be served by caterer
  of your choice
Space is very adaptable. Sprung maple floor,
  17' ceilings; needed scenic pieces can be supplied
Suggested uses: all special events are possible including an audition,
  video taping for commercials, photography shooting, or a
  chamber music concert

Vandam Theater, SoHo 242-2519
15 Vandam Street
New York, N.Y. 10013
Contact: Dorothy Ames

Auditorium/theater, rehearsal space, conference room,
  exhibit space, reception area
Seating capacity: 197 in auditorium; 70 in conference room
Stage, platform, dance floor; food may be served
Suggested uses: auction, concert, class, exhibit, lecture,
  meeting, performance

Village Gate 475-5120
160 Bleecker Street
New York, N.Y. 10012
Contact: Art D'Lugoff

2 cabaret theaters
Seating capacity: 300/450
Fully equipped stages, piano, dance floor, complete sound and
   lighting equipment, kitchen; food may be served by space
   or caterer of your choice
Suggested uses: concert, rehearsal, private party, off-Broadway
   presentation, location shooting

Vital Arts Center 675-1136
Eleo Pomare Dance Company
78 Fifth Avenue (btw. 13th & 14th Streets)
New York, N.Y. 10011
Contact: Virgil Akins

Performance/rehearsal space
Seating capacity: 100
Dance floor, dressing rooms, professional sound and lighting equipment

WPA Theater 691-2274
138 Fifth Avenue (at 19th Street, 2nd floor)
New York, N.Y. 10011
Contact: Kyle Renick

Theater, rehearsal space, green room
Seating capacity: 98 in theater; 26' x 33' of rehearsal space is available
Rental fee: $1,000 per week
26' x 33' proscenium stage

Ward-Nasse Gallery 925-6951
178 Prince Street
New York, N.Y. 10012
Contact: Maggie Reilly

Seating capacity: 100; 2500 sq. ft. of space is available
Rental fee: negotiable
Suggested uses: rehearsal, dance performance, poetry recital,
   small multi-media event

Westside Arts Theatre 246-6351
Chelsea Theatre Center
407 West 43rd Street
New York, N.Y. 10036
Contact: Steve Gilger, Theatre Manager

2 theatres, cabaret stage
Seating capacity: 199 in Downstairs Theatre (flexible seating);
   250 in Upstairs Theatre; 75 in cabaret
Rental fee: varies with production needs
Proscenium stage, thrust stage, platform, piano
Suggested uses: concert, class, professional dance, lecture,
   meeting, performance

The Westside Mainstage 664-9102
424 West 49th Street (Bate)
New York, N.Y. 10019 840-1234
Contact: Dana Bate or Don Silva (ans. service for Silva)

Performance space, rehearsal/meeting room
Seating capacity: 75 in performance space;
 50/65 in rehearsal space
Open stage, professional lighting equipment; food may be served
 by caterer of your choice
Space is in a renovated building which was a church

White Mask Theatre Corporation 683-9332
22 West 30th Street (btw. Fifth & Sixth Avenues, 3rd floor) 683-5557
New York, N.Y. 10001
Contact: Doloris Holmes, Director

Theatre in the round, rehearsal space, classroom, conference/
 meeting room, exhibit space
Seating capacity: 50/74
Rental fee: negotiable; $6.00 to $10.00 per hour for rehearsal space;
 $65 minimum per performance
Organ, dance floor, kitchen; food may be served on occasion
Suggested uses: all special events are possible except an auction,
 banquet, fair or reception

Also see: AUDITORIUMS
           CHURCHES
           LIBRARIES
           LOFTS
           MEETING ROOMS/CONFERENCE ROOMS/AUDITORIUMS (Seating 499 or less)
           PARKS & PLAZAS
           PERFORMANCE SPACES (Concert/Recital)
           PERFORMANCE SPACES (Dance/Theatre)
           SCHOOLS
           Y's

* * * * * * *

For the use of New York City Waterfront Recreation Sites
 contact in writing:

   Property Management Services
   N.Y.C. Department of Ports & Terminals
   Battery Maritime Building
   Foot of Whitehall Street
   New York, N.Y. 10004
   Attn: Sandy Carles

Available waterfront sites are:

   Pier 84, Manhattan
   Tiffany Street Pier, Bronx
   Mill Basin Bulkhead, Brooklyn
   Pier 13, Staten Island

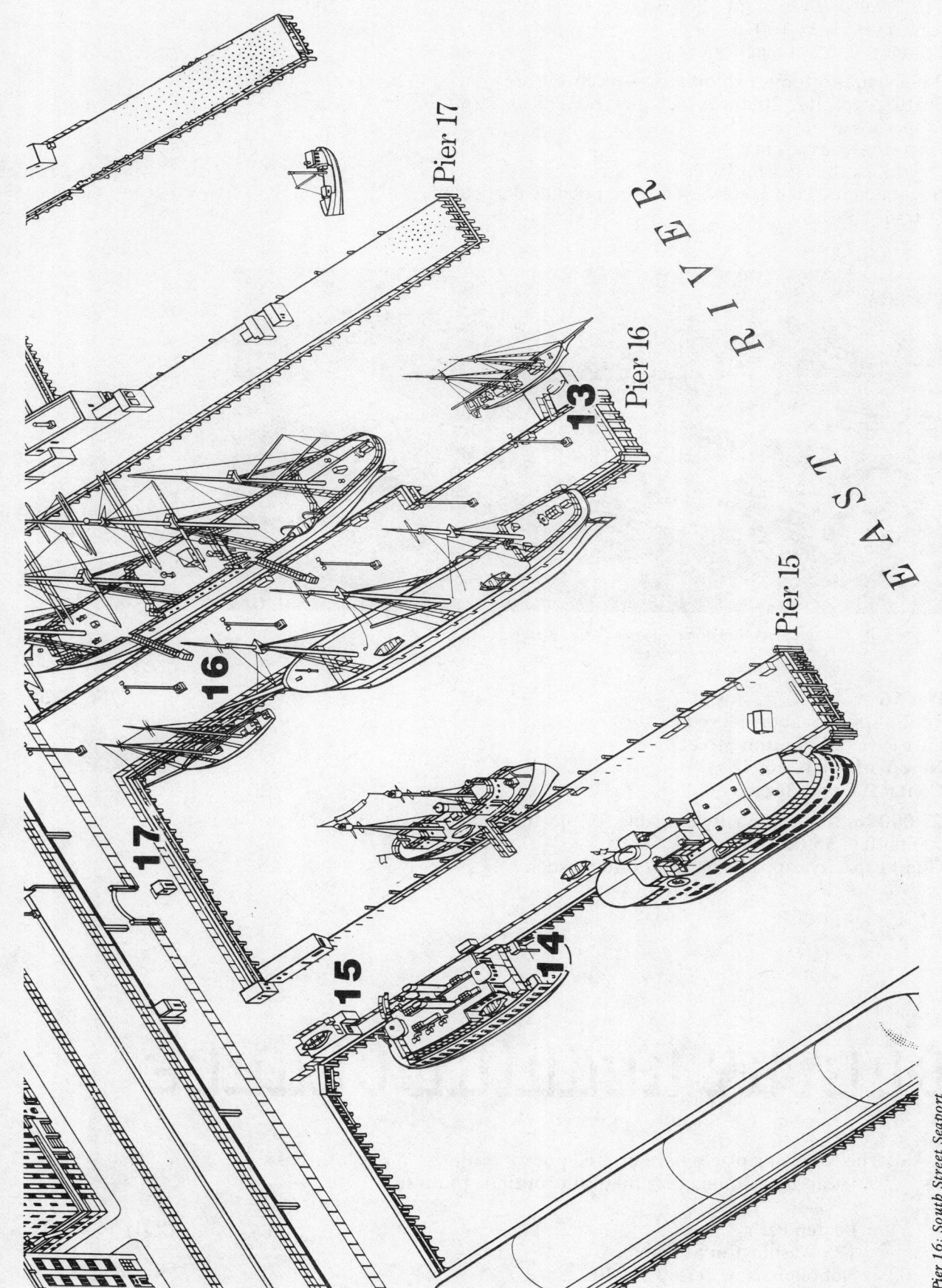

Pier 16: South Street Seaport

New York City Passenger Ship Terminal, Pier No. 92 466-7985
711 Twelfth Avenue (at 52nd Street)
New York, N.Y. 10019
Contact: Gloria Laughton

3 piers/auditoriums, exhibit space, reception area
Seating capacity: 2000 for each pier; 60,000 sq. ft. of pier space is available
Open rooftop parking
Overlooks the Hudson River
Suggested uses: all special events are possible particularly trade shows

Courtesy of: The Port Authority of New York and New Jersey

Pier 16 766-9020
South Street Seaport Museum
East River and Fulton Street
New York, N.Y. 10038
Contact: David Beggs

23,000 sq. ft. occasionally available for private functions
Rental fee: $5,000
Guest capacity: approximately 2,000 persons

****

POETRY READING PLACES

The following places have offered poetry readings on a regular basis. It can be assumed that they will continue to do so:

Beaten Path (201) 868-0239
125 Washington Street
Hoboken, New Jersey 07030

Books & Company 737-1450
939 Madison Avenue (btw. 74th & 75th Streets)
New York, N.Y. 10021

Charles Green Center 477-0666
Middle Collegiate Church
50 East 7th Street
New York, N.Y. 10023

Ear Inn, Inc. 226-9060
326 Spring Street
New York, N.Y. 10013

Eric 534-8500
1700 Second Avenue (at 88th Street)
New York, N.Y. 10028

Fashion Moda 585-0135
2803 Third Avenue
Bronx, N.Y. 10455

Galeria Morivivi 289-9332
1671 Lexington Avenue (at 95th Street)
New York, N.Y. 10028

Gallery Theatre 226-4167
SoHo 20
99 Spring Street
New York, N.Y. 10012

Guggenheim Museum 860-1356
1071 Fifth Avenue (btw. 88th & 89th Streets)
New York, N.Y. 10028

Le Figaro Cafe 677-1100
184 Bleecker Street
New York, N.Y. 10012

Newfoundland 255-4991
6 West 18th Street
New York, N.Y. 10011

Ohio 674-0910
The Open Space
64 Wooster Street
New York, N.Y. 10013

Poetry at St. Clement's Church 246-7277
423 West 46th Street
New York, N.Y. 10036

St. Mark's in the Bowery 674-0910
Poetry Project
131 East 10th Street
New York, N.Y. 10003

Womanbooks 874-4121
201 West 92nd Street
New York, N.Y. 10024

Also see: Association of Artist-Run Galleries
          Ward-Nasse Gallery

* * * * * * *

REHEARSAL PLACES

Abraham Goodman House
Actor's Playhouse
Actor's Repertory Theatre
Alum Dance Studio
American Academy and Institute
  of Arts and Letters
American Association of University Women
American Mime Theatre
Ansonia Hotel
Anthroposophical Society of America
The Barbizon
Barbizon Plaza Hotel
Beacon Theater
Bloomingdale House of Music
Bouwerie Lane Theater
Bronx House
The Buckley School
C.W. Post Center of Long Island
  University
Cami Hall
Caranci Studios
Carnegie Hall Corporation
Carnegie Recital Hall
Carter Theatre
Chelsea Hall
"Choreoground" and Dance Studios
Circle in the Square
City Center 55th Street Theater
Clark Center for the Performing Arts
Colonnades Theatre Lab, Inc.
Dance Theater Workshop
Dennis Wayne's Dancerschool Ltd.
Dramatis Personae
Drew Hamilton C.Y.O. Community Center
East Side International Community
  Center, Inc.
Eastern Christian Leasing Center
Edison Theater
Educational Alliance
Entermedia Theater
Fashion Institute of Technology
Fifth Avenue Hotel
Flushing Jewish Center (Queens)
42nd Street Theatre Row
Foundation for the Advance of Dance
Gene Frankl Theatre Workshop, Inc.
George Morrison Studios
George Tomov Studio
Greenwich House Music School
Guild Rehearsal Studios
Gustave Hartman YM-YWHA (Queens)
Harkness House
Harlequin Rehearsal Studio

Hotel Overlooking Gramercy Park
Hudson Guild
International House
Irish Arts Center
James Weldon Johnson Community
  Center
K & K Space & Toy Company
LaGuardia Community College (Queens)
Lehman College Center for the
  Performing Arts (Bronx)
Long Island University (Brooklyn)
Manhattan Punch Line Theatre
Manhattan School of Music
Manhattan Theater Club
Manhattanville Community Centers, Inc.
Marc Ballroom
Marymount Manhattan College
Merce Cunningham Studio
Metropolitan Republic Club
Sam & Esther Minskoff Cultural Center
Morris Mime Theatre
Mosholu-Montefiore Community Center
  (Bronx)
Nameless Theatre
Nat Horne Theatre
New Dramatists, Inc.
New Lincoln School
New York University/Loeb Student
  Center
Newfoundland
Nola Sound Studios, Inc.
Off Center Theatre
One Astor Place
The Palladium
Park Circle Roller Skating Rink
Pratt Institute
The Production Company
Queensborough Community College
Radio City Music Hall
Riverdale Country School (Bronx)
Riverdale-Yonkers Society for
  Ethical Culture
Roberto Clemente State Park (Bronx)
St. Hilda's & St. Hugh's School
Sloane House YMCA
Society for the Advancement of Judaism
Studio 58 Playhouse, Inc.
Studio of Creative Movement
Symphony Space
Theatre 22
Third Street Music School Settlement
Thirteenth Street Theater
Union Square Theatre

Vandam Theater, SoHo
Versatile Dance/Rehearsal Loft
 on West 21st Street
Vital Arts Center

WPA Theater
Ward-Nasse Gallery
White Mask Theatre Corporation
Workmen's Circle Building

* * * * * * *

(Roller and Ice Skating)

Coco's Disco Rink   675-3913
75 Christopher Street (off Sheridan Square)
New York, N.Y. 10014
Contact: Lew Voyles, Manager

450 people can be accommodated for a private skating party
Seating capacity: 5,000 sq. ft. of skating space is available;
 center of rink available for roller/disco dancing
3 lounges, live d.j., sound system, entertainment, snack bar;
 food available on premises or bring your own caterer
Located in what was a basement bowling alley, now there are mirrors and plants
Note: Alcohol is not allowed

Empire Roller Disco   462-1400
Empire Rollerdome
200 Empire Boulevard
Brooklyn, N.Y. 11225
Contact: Gloria McCarthy

2500 can be accommodated, 1500 skating/
 400 seated, in 2 skating rinks of 30,000 sq. ft.
Rental fee: approximately $4.00 per person
Sound equipment, flexible lighting, disco music, snack bar;
 food may be served
Note: Space is only available Monday evenings to private groups
 of 300 minimum

The Goodskates   877-1024
Mineral Springs Building
Sheep Meadow, Central Park
Contact: Judy Lynn, President

Private parties for up to 300 adults and/or 100 children
Skating to disco music in Mineral Springs Building courtyard
 and on paved roads in Central Park. The Goodskates also can
 arrange disco skating parties in your own home, cellar,
 school gymnasium, etc.
Group rates available
Refreshments may be served

Metropolis Roller Skate Club 586-8188
241 West 55th Street
New York, N.Y. 10019
Contact: Mario Courtney or Mark Soyka, Owners

1350 people may be accommodated; 100 in cafeteria
Rental fee: $20 per person for a private skating party for 150 minimum
Stage, platform, pro-shop, kitchen; food may be served
Suggested uses: all special events are possible except an auction, dance or fair
Note: Space requires 150 minimum for a skating party

Metropolis Roller Skate Club

Park Circle Roller Skating Rink 441-1889
11 Ocean Parkway
Brooklyn, N.Y. 11218
Contact: George Casey

1200 people may be accommodated
Rental fee: $4.00 per person for a private skating party
Disco sound system and lighting, floor guards, announcer; food may be served from space's concession
Suggested uses: exhibit, rehearsal, private skating party, private social and church functions, instruction
Note: Space requires 150 minimum for a skating party

The Roxy 691-3113
515 West 18th Street
New York, N.Y. 10009
Contact: Virginia Borghesan, Daytime Manager

1200 people can be accommodated
VIP area
Sound equipment, bar, restaurant; food may be served by space or caterer of your choice
Note: Monday is the preferred night for a private skating party

Sky Rink 695-6556
450 West 33rd Street
New York, N.Y. 10011
Contact: Howard Butler, Manager

Conference room/lounge
750 people may be accommodated; 150 in conference room
Music, snack bar, kitchen; food may be served
Suggested uses: banquet, meeting, party, ice skating performance, promotion, television commercial
Space is a penthouse atop a 16 story office building
Note: Space requires 27 minimum for a skating party

Village Skating 473-9200
15 Waverly Place (btw. Greene and Mercer)
New York, N.Y. 10003
Contact: Dick Clammer

Seating capacity: 100 for a private skating party
Music; food may be served by caterer of your choice
Rink is in the cellar of an old converted building near New York University

Also see: Branch Brook Skating Center and
South Mountain Arena (STADIUMS)

* * * * * * *

SCHOOLS & COLLEGES

Borough of Manhattan Community College 262-3443 (Dean)
Uris Building 262-5616 or
1633 Broadway (at 50th Street) 262-5446 (Secretary)
New York, N.Y. 10019
Contact: Dean of Administration or
Carmen Greenidge, Secretary

2 conference rooms
Seating capacity: 20/70
Note: Space is only available to non-profit groups

The Buckley School 535-8787
113 East 73rd Street
New York, N.Y. 10021
Contact: Per von Scheele

Gymnasium
Seating capacity: 40' x 70' of space is available
Note: Space is only available for sport activities

Fashion Institute of Technology

City College of the City University of New York 690-6900
134th Street & Convent Avenue
New York, N.Y. 10031
Contact: Joel Foster

> **Aaron Davis Hall**
> The Main Stage
> Seating capacity: 750
> 40' x 24' proscenium stage; 40' x 40'
>   performance sprung space
>
> **The Experimental Theatre**
> Seating capacity: 300 maximum
> 62' x 62' open space with full grid; sprung floor
> Rental fee: negotiable
> *Note:* Space has limited availability

Columbia University 280-5113
Earl Hall Center 280-3574
117th Street & Broadway
New York, N.Y. 10027
Contact: Irma Baez, Assistant Director

Auditorium, rehearsal space, ballroom, conference room,
  Room 302, meeting rooms, reception area (lobby)
Seating capacity: 150/250 in auditorium; 20/25 in conference
  room and Room 302; 75 in Dodge Room; 30/40 in Schiff Room;
  30 in lobby

> **Ferris Booth Hall** 280-3611
> Columbia University
> 115th Street & Broadway
> New York, N.Y. 10027
> Contact: Thomas Toronto, Operations Office, Room 206
>
> Seating capacity: 748 in Wollman Auditorium;
>   30/228 in 11 meeting rooms
>
> **Horace Mann Auditorium** 678-3707
> Columbia University Teachers College
> 525 West 120th Street
> New York, N.Y. 10027
> Contact: Rosemarie Amara, Director, Office of
>   Room Assignments
>
> Seating capacity: 650
> Stage, piano, organ, PA system, limited stage lighting
>
> **McMillan Theater** 280-2843
> Office of Community Affairs
> 313 Low Library, Columbia University
> New York, N.Y. 10027
> Contact: Glen Waggoner
>
> Seating capacity: 1200
>
> **Millbank Chapel** 678-3707
> Columbia University Teachers College
> 525 West 120th Street
> New York, N.Y. 10027
> Contact: Rosemarie Amara, Director, Office of
>   Room Assignments

Chapel, reception room, courtyard
Seating capacity: 200 in chapel; 80/90 in
   Grace Dodge Room

School of International Affairs Auditorium   280-2843
Office of Community Affairs
313 Low Library, Columbia University
New York, N.Y. 10027
Contact: Glen Waggoner

Seating capacity: 400

St. Paul's Chapel   280-5113
202 Earl Hall   280-3574
117th Street & Broadway
New York, N.Y. 10027
Contact: Irma Baez, Assistant Director

Nave, meeting room/lounge, reception area (Red Room)
Seating capacity: 500 in nave; 40 in Crypt lounge;
   75/100 in the Red Room

Cooper Union Great Hall   254-6300
Seventh Street & Third Avenue   ext. 205
New York, N.Y. 10003
Contact: Office of Continuing Education

Auditorium
Seating capacity: 900

The Dalton School   722-5160
108 East 89th Street
New York, N.Y. 10028
Contact: Business Office

Auditorium, reception rooms
Seating capacity: 424 in auditorium

Fashion Institute of Technology   760-7644
227 West 27th Street
New York, N.Y. 10001
Contact: Toni Lamont

Auditorium, rehearsal space, conference room, exhibit spaces
Amphitheatre, Board Room, Living Room, classrooms
Professional sound and lighting equipment
Seating capacity: 800 in Morris Haft Auditorium; 350 in
   Katie Murphy Amphitheatre

Marymount Manhattan College   472-3800
221 East 71st Street   ext. 474 for theater,
New York, N.Y. 10021   ext. 462 for other spaces
Contact: Director of College Events

Auditorium, rehearsal space, conference room, ballroom,
   reception area, classrooms, swimming pool
Seating capacity: 250 in theatre; 300 in ballroom; 100 in
   reception area; 20/60 in classrooms
Note: Space is only available to non-profit groups

The New Lincoln School 879-9200
210 East 77th Street
New York, N.Y. 10021
Contact: Myrtle Steele, Bursar

Rehearsal space, conference room, reception area
Seating capacity: 150

New York School of Printing 765-1185
439 West 49th Street
New York, N.Y. 10019
Contact: George Sikoryak, Custodian/Engineer

Auditorium
Seating capacity: 700

New York University 598-2022
Loeb Student Center
566 La Guardia Place (at Washington Square)
New York, N.Y. 10012
Contact: Operations Office, Room 300

Auditorium, meeting rooms, conference room, exhibit space,
   lounge, reception room, cafeteria, coffee house, checkroom
Seating capacity: varies

Pace University 285-3398
Schimmel Center for the Arts (for theater)
1 Pace Plaza
New York, N.Y. 10038 285-3624
Contact: Jess Adkins, Director; or Toni Small for other spaces (for other spaces)

Theater, conference room, reception area, meeting rooms,
   dining room, cafeteria
Seating capacity: 392 orchestra/276 balcony in auditorium;
   150/200 in other spaces

Parsons School of Design (Midtown Campus) 741-8959
560 Seventh Avenue (at 40th Street)
New York, N.Y. 10018
Contact: Terry Reynolds

Auditorium, conference rooms, exhibit space, reception area
Seating capacity: 15/450
Rental fee: varies with place and time
Suggested uses: catered breakfast, luncheon, cocktails, stock holders
   meeting, dance, fashion show, press or commencement showing,
   testimonial

PUBLIC SCHOOLS:

Space in Public School buildings:

   Note: Anyone wishing to use a classroom or auditorium
            of a public school after school hours, should get in
            touch with the Custodian of a specific school and
            request a permit application. (All public schools
            are listed in the telephone directory.) Rates will be

quoted by the Custodian from the schedule of rates
approved by the Board of Education. For additional
information contact:

Director of Plant Operations — 830-8802
Division of School Buildings
2811 Queens Plaza North
Long Island City, N.Y. 11101

Also see: AUDITORIUMS (Seating 500 or more)

St. Hilda's & St. Hugh's School — 666-9645
619 West 114th Street
New York, N.Y. 10025
Contact: Rev. Mother Ruth, Headmistress

Auditorium/gymnasium, rehearsal space, exhibit space, lounge
Seating capacity: 500

Village Community School — 691-5146
272 West Tenth Street
New York, N.Y. 10014
Contact: Sheila Sadler or Rudy Christian, Building Custodian

Auditorium, gymnasium
Seating capacity: 250

York Preparatory School — 628-1220
116 East 85th Street
New York, N.Y. 10028
Contact: R. Stewart

Auditorium, classrooms
Seating capacity: 110
Note: Entire school is available for long-term evening rental

BRONX:

Bronx Community College — 220-6260 (Freeberg)
West 181st Street & University Avenue
Bronx, N.Y. 10453 — 220-6450 (switchboard)
Contact: Ed Freeberg

Playhouse, 3 conference rooms
Seating capacity: 375 in Hall of Fame Playhouse;
up to 120 in each conference room
Rental fee: $60 per day plus technicians costs
Proscenium stage, pianos, professional sound and lighting
equipment; food may be served in places other than Playhouse
Suggested uses: banquet, concert, exhibit, lecture, meeting,
performance
Note: Space is usually only available to community groups

Lehman College Center for the Performing Arts — 960-8232
Bedford Park Boulevard West
Bronx, N.Y. 10468
Contact: Alan Light, Managing Director or
Valerie Simmons, Assistant Director

Concert hall (auditorium), theatre, experimental theatre (theatre in the round), rehearsal space, conference room, exhibit space, reception area, dining hall
Seating capacity: 2310 in concert hall; 500 in theatre; 200 in experimental theatre
Rental fee: $1,500 plus expenses for concert hall; $500 plus expenses for theatre; negotiable for experimental theatre
Stage, proscenium stage, piano, dance floor, complete fly system for scenery and lighting equipment, kitchen; food may be served
All special events are possible except a social dance, fair, party or wedding
Note: This is a newly developed performance space

Riverdale Country School 549-8810
5250 Fieldston Road
Bronx, N.Y. 10471
Contact: Barbara Lesser

Auditorium, rehearsal space, conference room, gymnasium, baseball field; catering is available
Seating capacity: approximately 250

>246th Street & Palisades Avenue
>Bronx, N.Y. 10471

>Auditorium, classrooms, gymnasium, baseball field, tennis courts; catering is available
>Seating capacity: approximately 150

Also see: College of Mount St. Vincent

BROOKLYN:

Adelphi Academy 238-3308
8515 Ridge Boulevard
Brooklyn, N.Y. 11209
Contact: Dean Hansen

Auditorium, gymnasium, classrooms
Seating capacity: 200 in auditorium; 20 in each classroom
Note: Space has limited availability except during the summer

Long Island University — Brooklyn Center 834-6095
1 University Plaza
Brooklyn, N.Y. 11201
Contact: Sally Castiglione, Special Events

Auditorium, theatre, classrooms, gymnasium, athletic field, exhibit space, gallery areas, reception area, lecture halls, dining rooms
Seating capacity: 550 in auditorium; 90/150 in lecture halls; 60/250 in dining rooms

QUEENS & LONG ISLAND:

C.W. Post Center of Long Island University (516) 299-2781
P.O. Greenvale, N.Y. 11548 (516) 299-2782
Contact: Peg Larsen

Concert Theater, 2 auditoriums, rehearsal space, conference
   rooms, exhibit space, Interfaith Chapel
Seating capacity: 2700 in Concert Theater; 40/500 in other spaces

Hofstra University   (516) 560-3281
Hempstead, N.Y. 11550
Contact: Dr. Donald H. Swinney, Director of Playhouse

Auditorium (John Cranford Adams Playhouse)
Seating capacity: 1134

Iona College   (914) 636-2100
715 North Avenue   ext. 419
New Rochelle, N.Y. 10801
Contact: Michael Schultz

Auditorium, classrooms, gymnasium, exhibit space
Seating capacity: 300 in auditorium; 40 in classrooms;
   4,000 in 180' x 120' gymnasium

LaGuardia Community College   626-5053
City University of New York
31-10 Thomson Avenue
Long Island City, N.Y. 11101
Contact: Eileen Mentone, Director of Community Relations

Auditorium, rehearsal space, conference room, exhibit space,
   reception area, classrooms, gymnasium, faculty dining room, terrace
Seating capacity: 250 in auditorium; 35 in conference room;
   15/80 in classrooms

Queens College   520-7200
Long Island Expressway & Kissena Boulevard   (Colden Center)
Flushing, N.Y. 11367   520-7609
Contact: Caroline Werth for Colden Center or   (Ferrar)
   Lawrence Ferrar, Campus Facilities Officer for other spaces

2 theatre spaces, lounges, gymnasium, athletic fields; cafeterias
Seating capacity: 2143 in Colden Center; 500 in QC Theatre; 320 Rathaus Recital Hall

Queens College Student Union   520-7800
152-45 Melbourne Avenue
Flushing, N.Y. 11367
Contact: Todd Edelman

Ballroom, 14 conference rooms, exhibit space, lounges,
   underground parking
Seating capacity: 600 in Grand Ballroom

Queensborough Community College   631-6321
56th Avenue & Springfield Boulevard   (Carobine)
Bayside, N.Y. 11365   631-6228
Contact: Tony Carobine, Director of Performing Arts   (Lundenberg)
   or Arnold Lundenberg, Campus Planning

Auditorium/theater, rehearsal space, conference room, plaza,
   exhibit space, reception area, 2 dressing rooms
Seating capacity: 871 in auditorium
Rental fee: $600 per performance
40' x 30' x 21' proscenium stage, platform, piano, complete
   sound and lighting equipment
Suggested uses: auction, concert, class, lecture, meeting,
   performance, reception

STATEN ISLAND:

The College of Staten Island   390-7949
Sunnyside Campus
715 Ocean Terrace
Staten Island, N.Y. 10301
Contact: Dr. Harold Taylor, Director of Office of External Affairs

Auditorium, quadrangle, sports field, parking lot
Seating capacity: 918 in Williamson Theatre
Stage, platform, piano, kitchen; space's cafeteria food only
   may be served

      St. George Campus
      130 Stuyvesant Place
      Staten Island, N.Y. 10301

      College hall
      Seating capacity: 175
      Stage, platform, piano; space's cafeteria food only
         may be served

Eltingville Lutheran School   984-8830
300 Genessee Avenue
Staten Island, N.Y. 10312
Contact: Priscilla Dahl

Church parlor, playground
Seating capacity: 150

Wagner College   390-3221
631 Howard Avenue
Staten Island, N.Y. 10301
Contact: Roger Solberg

Auditorium, conference rooms, gymnasium, exhibit space,
   reception area, cafeteria
Seating capacity: 320 in auditorium; 14/85 in conference room;
   1650 in gymnasium; 400 in Main Cafeteria

SCHOOLS: IN THE VICINITY OF N.Y.C.

Bard College   (914) 758-6822
Annandale-on-Hudson, N.Y. 12504
Contact: Sue T. Crane, Director of Summer Programs

Conference space, rehearsal space, exhibit space, reception area,
   gymnasium, game room, dining room, mansion
Seating capacity: 150 in performance/lecture halls; 25/75 in
   conference room; 200 in reception area; 800 in gymnasium;
   25/75 in studio spaces; 100 in Blithewood Mansion

Fairleigh Dickinson University (201) 377-4700
Fordham-Madison Campus ext. 357
Madison, N.J. 07940
Contact: Special Events Manager

This 187 acre campus is the site of the former Twombly Estate,
  owned by Florence Vanderbilt Twombly and Hamilton Twombly.
Lenfell Hall is located in the 100 room mansion now used as the
  college administration building. The Hall was once the grand
  ballroom of the estate.
Guest capacity: 250 sitdown/600 for cocktails in Lenfell Hall
  (adjoining gardens may also be used for special functions);
  20 in Sullivan Lounge (at a mahagony table); 50/60 in
  Hartman Lounge (a panelled room)
Suggested uses: concert, lecture, reception, formal dinner dance

Fairleigh Dickinson University

Manhattanville College (914) 694-2200
Purchase, N.Y. 10577
Contact: Marie DeMarco, Facilities Supervisor or Sr. Rennee (for weddings only)

Theater, ballroom, classrooms, reception space
Seating capacity: 120 in Little Theater; 500 in East Room;
  20/120 in classrooms
Rental fee: varies
Caterer is available
Suggested uses: banquet, meeting, conference, performance, wedding

Marymount College (914) 631-3200
Neperan Road ext. 209
Tarrytown, N.Y. 10591
Contact: Sr. George Ellen, Coordinator of Services
  and Programming

Auditorium, theatre/concert hall, classrooms, conference rooms,
  exhibit space, lecture hall, dining room
Seating capacity: 953 in auditorium, 225 in lecture hall;
  149 in theatre; 30 in classrooms; 1,000 in dining room
Stage, piano; food may be served only by space's own caterer
Suggested uses: all special events are possible including a
  wedding reception

William Paterson College Student Center
300 Pompton Road
Wayne, N.J. 07470
Contact: Sharon Kinder, Special Events Coordinator

(201) 595-2292
ext. 33 or 47

Ballroom/multi-purpose room, 3 conference rooms,
 4 meeting rooms, exhibit space, 3 lounges, dining room,
 recreation area, 2 terraces, parking lot
Seating capacity: 400 in ballroom; 10/40 in each conference room;
 12/25 in each meeting room; 35/60 in each lounge

Also see: AUDITORIUMS (Seating 500 or more)
 CONFERENCE CENTERS

****

SCREENING ROOMS

Eleonora
117 West 58th Street
New York, N.Y. 10019
Contact: Joseph Lyttle, Proprietor

765-1427
765-1438

Film and TV cassette screening room is part of this Italian restaurant
Seating capacity: 20
Restaurant's own food and drink may be served

Magno Park Avenue Screening Room
445 Park Avenue (btw. 56th & 57th Streets)
New York, N.Y. 10022
Contact: Ralph Friedman or Maria Pon

757-8855

Screening room
Seating capacity: 40
16mm and 35mm interlock and composite screening,
 video screening

Magno Penthouse Screening Room
1540 Broadway (at 45th Street)
New York, N.Y. 10036

Seating capacity: 40/50
16mm and 35mm multi-track screening

Magno Preview
1600 Broadway (at 48th Street)
New York, N.Y. 10019

Screening rooms, editing rooms
Seating capacity: 12/75
Editing equipment, equipment maintenance

Magno Sound and Video
212 West 48th Street
New York, N.Y. 10022

Mixing, transfers, stripping, codings, voice recording,
 sound effects, video

Rizzoli Editore Corporation　　　　　　　　　　　　　　　　　　397-3738
Rizzoli Screening Room
712 Fifth Avenue (at 56th Street)
New York, N.Y. 10019
Contact: Mary Albano

Screening room
Seating capacity: 50
Rental fee: varies from $65 to $75 per hour
Motion picture projector, sound equipment, 35mm and 16mm
　　interlock screening

Also see: LIBRARIES

* * * * * * *

STADIUMS

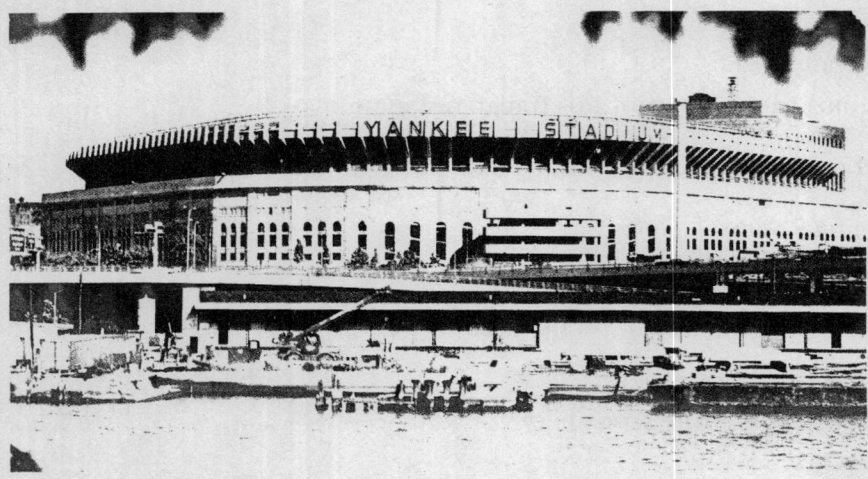

John J. Downing Stadium	stadium: 860-1830
Randall's Island, Manhattan	permit: 397-3116
Seating capacity: 20,000	

Essex County Department of Parks, Recreation　　　(201) 483-2088
　and Cultural Affairs　　　　　　　　　　　　　　　(Branchbrook)
115 Clinton Avenue　　　　　　　　　　　　　　　　(201) 482-6400
Newark, N.J. 07104　　　　　　　　　　　　　　　　(switchboard)
Contact: Robert Hudson

　Branch Brook Skating Center
　Branch Brook Park
　Newark, N.J. 07104

　Seating capacity: 700 grandstand/2000 folding chairs
　　in 225' x 122' building with a 40' ceiling
　Parking lot can accommodate 400 automobiles
　30 minutes from New York City

South Mountain Arena
560 Northfield Avenue
West Orange, N.J. 07052
Contact: Carl DeLuca, Manager

(201) 731-3829
(South Mountain)
(201) 482-6400
(switchboard)

Meeting/conference room
Seating capacity: 2640 permanent seats/1400 folding chairs
   in 248' x 148' building with a 60' ceiling
In-house organ, theatrical lighting, large parking lot
One hour from New York City

Both of these facilities have a 200' x 85' indoor ice skating
   rink (surface can be converted), fully equipped PA
   systems, control booths, locker rooms, and luncheonettes.
   Additional personnel are available. Suitable for all special
   events including a circus, tennis exhibition, sports
   competition, trade show, convention, horse show

Giant Stadium
New Jersey Sports Exposition Authority
East Rutherford, New Jersey 07073
Seating capacity: 76,981

stadium: (201) 935-8500
ext. 4387

Madison Square Garden Center
4 Pennsylvania Plaza
New York, N.Y. 10001
Contact: Alvin Grant

563-8000

Forum-amphitheater seats 4600
Madison Square Garden — major sports event, convention,
   entertainment spectacular; seats 20,000
Penn Plaza Club — Dining area and cocktail lounge
Rotunda — 50,000 sq. ft. exposition area
Bowling Center, Press Club
Catered food may be served
Suggested uses: anniversary, film, sales meeting, exposition,
   commencement program, symposium, alumni gathering, clinic,
   dining, etc.

Nassau Veterans Memorial Coliseum
Mitchel Field Complex
Uniondale, N.Y. 11553
Contact: Antoni Travars, Executive Director
   for arena and exhibit hall or Harry M.
   Stevens, Inc. for kitchen and food

(516) 794-9300
(arena)
(516) 794-3555
(restaurant and concession services)

Arena/auditorium, exhibit hall
Seating capacity: 17,000 maximum in arena
Rental fee: $8500 or 17½% of gross ticket receipts plus
   expenses, whichever is greater per event, for arena;
   30,000 sq. ft. minimum at 4 cents per gross sq. ft. or
   17½% of gross ticket receipts, whichever is greater
   per event, for exhibit hall
Proscenium stage, platform, kitchen; food may be served
   only by space's own caterer
Suggested uses: banquet, concert, exhibit, consumer and trade shows

Rice Stadium
Pelham Bay Park, Bruckner Blvd. &
   Middletown Road, Bronx
Seating capacity: 4500

stadium: 822-4288
permit: 822-4598

Shea Municipal Stadium
Flushing Meadows — Corona Park, Queens
Seating capacity: 55,000

stadium: 699-4220
permit: 360-8153

U.S. Tennis Association National Tennis Center
Flushing Meadow Park, Queens
Flushing, N.Y. 11368
Seating capacity: 19,000

stadium: 592-8000
permit: 592-8000

Van Cortlandt Park Stadium
West 241st Street and Broadway, Bronx
Seating capacity: 3600

stadium: 548-9679
permit: 822-4598

Yankee Stadium
River Avenue & 161st Street, Bronx
Seating capacity: 55,000

stadium: 293-4300
permit: 566-1032

Also see: SCHOOLS & COLLEGES

* * * * * * *

STEPS

In a formal sense, steps leading to public buildings can be used for public ceremonies and press conferences. Informally, they serve as places for sunbathing, people watching, impromptu concerts and rendezvous perches for meeting friends. Some of the best steps for these purposes are those of the Low Memorial Library at Columbia University, the Metropolitan Museum of Art, St. Thomas Church, St. Patrick's Cathedral, The New York Public Library at Fifth Avenue and 42nd Street, City Hall and Federal Hall.

Steps at the Metropolitan Museum of Art

* * * * * * *

STUDIO SPACES

Department of General Services 566-7489
Division of Real Property (Metaxas)
2 Lafayette Street
New York, N.Y. 10007 233-2926
Contact: Takis J. Metaxas, Director of Community Leasing or (Dixey)
   Zoe Dixey, Community Liaison for Operation Green Thumb

Any non-profit group in search of permanent studio and/or workshop space may write to the above address and contact person. The letter should give proof of the group's non-profit status and intended use of property. A letter of support from the Community Board where property is located will be requested; if a cultural group, a letter of support from Department of Cultural Affairs, if for one-time event or outdoor festival a letter of approval from Police Precinct commander having jurisdiction where property is located. A certified financial statement detailing funding and demonstrating, when a structure is involved, capability to provide for maintenance and operating expenses.

All city-owned property, such as police and fire stations, vacant school buildings, etc., may be leased to a service-oriented, non-profit group on a month to month lease agreement. The group must provide its own insurance, pay utilities, and be prepared to move out of the premises if and when a city agency wants occupancy. Rent is the fair market value.

Under Operation Green Thumb city-owned lots throughout the five boroughs are leased to community residents for $1.00 a year to be developed into urban gardens. Technical assistance, seeds, soil and tools, will be provided whenever possible. Insurance is not required.

If a group is not certain as to whether a specific space is city-owned, Director Metaxas will check it out.

For information on the multi-use of school buildings see the listing under PUBLIC SCHOOLS.

The Downtown Cultural Center 570-3651
48 Old Slip
New York, N.Y. 10004
Contact: David Hubert, Whitney Museum Education Department

Performance space, small exhibition spaces, studio space, office space
Seating capacity: 100 in performance space
Facility is housed in the former First Precinct Building built in 1901
Studio space is only available to individual artists during June, July and August; office space is only available to arts organizations that provide a cultural service to Lower Manhattan

Institute for Art and Urban Resources, Inc. 784-2084
c/o Project Studio One (P.S. 1)
46-01 21st Street
Long Island City, N.Y. 11101
Contact: Allana Heiss, President and Executive Director

Auditorium, 20 studios
Seating capacity: 8000 sq. ft. of exhibit and performance space
  is available
Rental fee: Applicable only when studio/workspace is rented for
  a period of up to a year. There is no rental fee for use of exhibit
  or performance space. Performance space and special project
  space is given by submission of a proposal in writing. All
  exhibition areas are curated
Space was a 19th century school building which has been
  converted into an experimental work center for artists

Project Studios One, P.S. 1

Jamaica Arts Center   658-7400
161-04 Jamaica Avenue
Jamaica, N.Y. 11432
Contact: Carol Argroe

Exhibit space, meeting rooms, performing and visual arts studio space
Seating capacity: 150
Rental fee: approximately $25 during the evening; negotiable
  flat fee for regular use
Piano; food may be served
Note: Collections and admission charges are usually not allowed

Inter-Media Art Center, Inc.   (516) 628-8585
253 Bayville Avenue
Bayville, N.Y. 11709
Contact: Michael Rothbard, Executive Director

50' x 50' color television studio, ¾" plus ½" formats, with
  editing facilities for video tape production
Rental fee: $25 per hour for studio production; $20 per hour
  for editing facilities
Note: Space is only available by application. Non-profit groups
  and independent artists are particularly welcome

Multi-use of Public School Buildings   830-8888
2811 Queens Plaza North
Long Island City, N.Y. 11101
Contact: Geraldine Prishivalco, Multi-Use Coordinator,
  Bureau of Space Programming, Management & Utilization

When a school facility is under-utilized by the school at the time
  the school is in-session, space may be available on a permanent
  basis to qualified non-profit, educational and service-oriented groups.

Organization of Independent Artists   929-6688
201 Varick Street
New York, N.Y. 10014
Contact: Warren Tanner

This organization facilitates visual art exhibitions such as painting,
   sculpture and photography. Information on the use of federal
   properties for cultural purposes and the Public Building Co-
   operative Use Act is available.

The Writer's Room
8 West 48th Street
New York, N.Y. 10018
Contact: Abby Schaefer

13 spaces are available to writers
Rental fee: $100 per three month period
Writers must demonstrate their seriousness and need for
   a regular work space. Requests must be made in writing.
   There is a waiting list.

* * * * * * *

Note: For **TOWNHOUSES** see: **MEETING ROOMS/CONFERENCE ROOMS/**
                            AUDITORIUMS (seating 499 or less)
                          PRIVATE PARTIES/PRIVATE PLACES
                          PRIVATE PARTIES/PUBLIC PLACES

For **WEDDINGS & WEDDING RECEPTIONS** see:
                BALLROOMS
                BOATS, BARGES & BALLOONS
                CHURCHES
                DISCOS & SUPPERCLUBS
                HOTELS
                LOFTS
                MEETING ROOMS/CONFERENCE ROOMS/
                      AUDITORIUMS (seating 499 or less)
                PARKS
                PRIVATE PARTIES/Private Places
                SCHOOLS & COLLEGES

MANHATTAN:

92nd Street YM-YWHA   427-6000
1395 Lexington Avenue   ext. 220
New York, N.Y. 10028
Contact: Linda Greenberg

Auditorium/concert hall
Seating capacity: 916

Sloane House YMCA 760-5860
356 West 34th Street
New York, N.Y. 10001
Contact: Valerie Henry

Auditorium, rehearsal space, conference rooms, lounge,
  exhibit space
Seating capacity: 200 in auditorium; 15/80 in conference rooms

Vanderbilt YMCA 755-2410
224 East 47th Street
New York, N.Y. 10017
Contact: Kathy Vaugn or Chuck Accurso, Membership
  Public Relations Director

Conference rooms
Seating capacity: 12/100

Westside YMCA 787-4400
Adult Education Department ext. 116
5 West 63rd Street
New York, N.Y. 10023
Contact: Joyce Portney

5 conference rooms, 3 classrooms, cafeteria
Seating capacity: 12/75
Rental fee: $20 to $40 for a half day; $50 to $70 for whole day

Young Men's Christian Association, McBurney Branch 741-9221
215 West 23rd Street
New York, N.Y. 10011
Contact: Dan Ruderman, Adult Program Director or
  Tom Bynum, Assistant

Auditorium, conference room, 7 meeting rooms, gymnasium,
  pool, running track
Seating capacity: 225 in auditorium; 120 in conference room;
  25/70 in meeting rooms

BROOKLYN:

Brooklyn YWCA 875-1190
30 Third Avenue
Brooklyn, N.Y. 11217
Contact: Alice Howard, Building Office

Auditorium (Memorial Hall), conference room, ballroom, exhibit space,
  gymnasium, pool
Seating capacity: 438 main floor/167 balcony in auditorium
Rental fee: $200 for 4 hours in auditorium plus $25 set up and
  maintenance; $25 for kitchen

East Flatbush Rugby Y 495-6000
555 Remsen Avenue
Brooklyn, N.Y. 11236
Contact: Lillian Schwartz

Conference room, gymnasium
Seating capacity: 150 in conference room; 350 in gymnasium

Gustave Hartman YM-YWHA 471-0200
710 Hartman Lane
Far Rockaway, N.Y. 11691
Contact: Steven Kaplansky, Executive Director

Auditorium, rehearsal space, conference room, playground,
  exhibit space, lounge, game room, parking lot
Seating capacity: 270

QUEENS:

Central Queens YMCA 739-6600
89-25 Parsons Boulevard
Jamaica, N.Y. 11432
Contact: Janet Sumers, Executive Director

6 meeting rooms, 2 gymnasiums, large swimming pool
Seating capacity: 70 in each meeting room; 35/70 in each gymnasium;
  40 in pool
Piano; food may be served by caterer of your choice
Suggested uses: class, dance, exhibit, lecture, meeting, party,
  church service

YM-YWHA of Greater Flushing 461-3030
Dora & Abraham Felt Building
45-35 Kissena Boulevard
Flushing, N.Y. 11355
Contact: Anne Jensky

Auditorium, conference room, 3 clubrooms
Seating capacity: 250 in auditorium; 15/30 in each classroom

* * * * * * *

PARTIES

AN INTRODUCTION TO THINGS OF VALUE
AND THEIR IMAGINATIVE RE-USE

The set designers of Columbia Pictures needed a mansion for shooting "Annie." Not just any mansion would do. This one had to house the film's eccentric billionaire Daddy Warbucks. For months nothing appropriate turned up. The best houses had either become museums or had already appeared in too many other films. Finally a 130 room palace of marble, with 1,500 mirrors, a billiard room, a theater seating 300, two bowling alleys and an indoor swimming pool was found on the campus of a private college in West Long Branch, New Jersey. Originally, designed in the 1920's by Horace Trumbauer for Herbert T. Parson, president of the F.W. Woolworth Company, who later lost it for non-payment of taxes, *Shadow Lawn*, as the mansion is called, had to take in other tenants, a military academy, a military hospital and a school for girls; until it was bought by Monmouth College to be used as an administration building.

It was just a question of time before another grand mansion would be junked in Norwalk, Connecticut. Its pipes had burst, its roof had fallen in, its original furniture had been sold at auction as long ago as the 1870's and its gardens had been taken over by a police station, an asphalt parking lot and a sand-and-gravel operation. Built in 1868 for LeGrand Lockwood, a man who had become rich and later poor by the stock market, this about-to-be-sold for scrap heap of grandeur was nevertheless called by former Secretary of the Interior, Roger C.B. Morton "the most sumptuous private home built in America up to that time" and "a prelude to the opulence of the Gilded Age."

The story of these two mansions, *Shadow Lawn*, in New Jersey and *The Lockwood-Mathews Mansion* in Connecticut, can be shared by many others across the country. Built by 19th century industrial tycoons, their Grand Halls and stairways, foyers, rotundas and Venetian glass ceilings; their breakfast rooms, billiard rooms, salons and ballrooms; their greenhouses, tennis courts, and gazebos incorporated every mood and style of design—for the taste of the Captains of Industry was exuberantly *laissez-faire*. Moorish, Pompeiian, Byzantine, French, English Tudor, Italian Renaissance and Chinese were all part of an architectural appetite served "banquet style."

Shadow Lawn

Lockwood-Mathews Mansion

But in a country of rapid changes, the fortunes of these sons of the Industrial Revolution changed too. And even if they didn't, the times changed. Ironically, the advocates of consumption and obsolescence seemed to reap what they sowed, for by the 1930's, '40's and '50's, there was hardly an American community that didn't have its "white elephant"—a shuttered mansion whose master and family had gone. And, in order to avoid the wrecker's ball, these *grand dames* of stone and gilt had to allow their indoor swimming pools to be used for storage of office supplies, their master bedrooms to be partitioned into dormitories for the mentally ill, the homeless and the unwed. But even the transformation of their grand salons into undertaking parlors was to be preferred to non-occupancy, which meant abandonment and inevitably led to vandalism, plunder and rape.

The story "From Prince to Frog" has a new installment now: The raising of consciousness which has touched so many areas in the recent past has also nudged our perceptions of history and values through architecture. For example, just before the *Lockwood-Mathews* mansion in Norwalk was to be razed, a citizen's Common Interest Group was formed to preserve it. By 1971, the mansion was designated a National Registered Landmark and when Mayor William Collins recently got married there, it came full circle—for mansions such as *Shadow Lawn* are in themselves a celebration—as statements that life, indeed, was good to their original owners. But even if most of us today see no cause to celebrate a lifetime of bonanza, each one of us has moments in our individual lives that call for special celebrations—be it a wedding, an anniversary, an award, and in the case of business, any number of important occasions.

Of course, grand estates and mansions are not the only category of imaginative re-use. Old canneries and railway stations, button manufacturing sweatshops, etc., are being reclaimed too. Thus, not only the residence of the industrial tycoon, but also the very place of his manufacture is a prospect for reclamation.

In Paterson, New Jersey for example, The Great Falls Development Corporation is restoring an impressive number of 18th century factories at the very site where they originally stood when they gave birth to the Industrial Revolution on the North American continent. The magnificently restored *Rogers Locomotive Works*, for example, serves as a grand exhibition hall as well as for professional offices and studios for artists on the very spot of the Passaic River which caused Alexander Hamilton to envision a great manufacturing center and a great nation.

Rogers Locomotive Works

And in New York City, where former industrial buildings give no hint of elegance from the outside, their sweep of space and light, claimed from a sweatshop where foreign-born hunched over rows of sewing machines, is elegance, indoors. High-ceilinged, with 40 windows overlooking the New York skyline, columns standing: the loft, a space re-claimed, sets the stage for celebrations.

Thus, PLACES is pleased to be able to include for the first time a nationwide sampling of "places reclaimed." All are available for special functions, all breathe of a time past, and all gracefully and magnificently serve the present, giving us a dimension few newer buildings can duplicate. Also, in so doing, an economic base is forged for the continued restoration and maintenance of these once-upon-a-time environments.

Instead of the bulldozer and the garbage heap, perceiving both beauty and new function in what no longer serves its original purpose and seeing to it that it is brought into the mainstream of the present, thus enriching us all, is truly visionary.

The Publishers

A Baronial Mansion

PRIVATE PARTY/ PRIVATE PLACES

(in New York City)

Abundance 737-7536
Staten Island, N.Y.

110-year-old Queen Anne Victorian building with fireplace and porch

Gourmet natural food may be served only by caterer on premises for an elegant dinner or picnic lunch. 50 people may be accommodated for a buffet/25 for sitdown dining; 25/35 on porch and alongside house

Suggested uses: dinner or brunch party

Abundance

A Baronial Mansion, Reborn 737-7536
(Lower East Side near Gramercy Park)
New York, N.Y.

Built in the 1860's by an English baron and having fallen on hard times through the years, this stately mansion and garden has been lovingly restored by its new owner

Lavishly furnished Louis XV Ballroom and Grand Salon, Spanish and Italian Renaissance reception rooms, its two chandeliered floors offer party elegance of a bygone era

Creative Space near Central Park 737-7536
New York, N.Y.

Situated in a turn-of-the-century brownstone in the West 70's half a block from Central Park, this very private and newly renovated space offers two floors connected by a modern staircase, partially brick-exposed walls for art exhibitions, flood and spot lighting, large French windows overlooking private gardens, a working fireplace and wall-to-wall carpeting with matching banquettes

Slide and film projection also available. Tuxedoed doorman and red carpet upon request.

Guest capacity: 100 maximum for buffet-style functions

Complete kitchen facility

Suggested uses: exhibition, promotion, film screening, fashion photography, wedding reception, surprise birthday party and various other private celebrations

Creative Space Near Central Park

Designer Loft In SoHo
New York, N.Y.

737-7536

Already favored by persons in the performing arts, this 2000 sq. ft. light and airy loft is decorated with art work and a poetry collection

Guest capacity: maximum of 60 sitdown; 125 for a buffet; 175 for cocktails

Grand piano

Designer Loft in SoHo

East 63rd Street Townhouse Floor
New York, N.Y.
737-7536

This upper Eastside home of a caterer with brick walls, chandeliers, a bar and dance floor, was especially designed with parties in mind

Elegant "French Bistro" Loft

Elegant "French Bistro" Loft
New York, N.Y.
737-7536

Softly hued "French Bistro" decor gives this living loft a classy/ comfortable mood. Glass panels from a patisserie in Paris set the ambience of the main party room. In addition, a separate bar area complete with zinc top bar from Lyon add to the loft's uniqueness.

Located in Chelsea in the shadow of The Fashion Institute of Technology, there is convenient parking.

100 for cocktails; 80 to 100 for buffet; 40 to 50 for sit-down dining
Caterer on premises or bring your own

The Faculty House

The Faculty House
Columbia University
New York, N.Y.
737-7536

Built in 1923 of Harvard brick with limestone base, this twin
   structure to The President's House offers three floors of
   dining and meeting rooms for small and large functions
Guest capacity: up to 250 on each floor; 700 if all 3 floors
   are used
Small private dining/meeting rooms are also available
Suitable for all manner of social functions including a wedding,
   conference or dinner meeting

Fin de Siècle Intimacy in Spacious Interior   737-7536
New York, N.Y.

Exquisite turn-of-the-century antiques are artfully arranged
   into numerous private islands giving this 6000 sq. ft. space
   an entirely un-barnlike interior
Thirty-nine tall windows offer dramatic views of the Empire State,
   Con Edison, Metropolitan Life and Chrysler Buildings lit up at night
Located on Fifth Avenue near Gramercy Park, this is one of the most
   extraordinary private party spaces in the City
300 for cocktails; 225 for buffet; 125 sit-down dinner
Caterer on premises

Georgian Suite   737-7536
(East 77th Street)
New York, N.Y.

Private suite
Seating capacity: 200 for cocktails/100 sitdown and dancing
Rental fee: negotiable
Dance floor, food may be served by space's own caterer only
Arches separate dinner and dancing sections; formal decor
Suggested uses: small auction, formal social activity

Gracious Murray Hill Brownstone   737-7536
New York, N.Y.

Tall windows with a garden view, book-lined study, fireplace,
   musician's own grand piano, and a full kitchen make this
   tastefully decorated and centrally located city residence
   a special place for quiet gatherings
Guest capacity: 50/75 maximum. Suitable for smaller groups
   as well
Suggested uses: literary party, music recital, small corporate gatherings
   promotion, small wedding, cocktail party or reception

Harkness House   794-0203
4 East 75th Street
New York, N.Y. 10021
Contact: Nikita Talin, Executive Director, or
   Theodore Bartwink, Controller

Rehearsal space, conference room, ballroom, exhibit/gallery space
Seating capacity: approximately 200 in ballroom
Piano, dance floor, kitchen; food may be served by caterer of your choice
Suggested uses: auction, banquet, class, exhibit, lecture, meeting,
   party, reception, wedding

Living Loft of A Caterer and An Indoor Landscaper
New York, N.Y.

737-7536

In the vicinity of the new Convention Center, this architecturally designed 2,500 ft. L—shaped, light and airy space offers 20 windows, a gourmet kitchen, built-in buffet area, an art deco lobby and the combined talents of the owners, i.e., visually appealing food and large, living plants

Guest capacity: 60 sitdown with room for dancing; 125 for cocktails

Although caterer is on premises, you may bring your own
Ample parking is available

Living Loft of A Caterer and An Indoor Landscaper

Movie-Set Loft
(Broadway & Bleecker Streets)
New York, N.Y.

737-7536

This sleekly modern 4000 sq. ft. art loft in the Village/SoHo area is often used as a set for motion picture, television and still photography. Featuring a 25 ft. red oak bar, fireplace, open kitchen, 11 ft. ceilings, arched windows and constantly changing art shows, it makes a chic New York party setting.

150 guests for cocktails; 100 for buffet or sit-down dining.

Caterer available or bring your own.

Movie-Set Loft

Murray Hill Townhouse
New York, N.Y.

737-7536

This private brownstone in the heart of New York's historic
  Murray Hill combines the charm and elegance of 1881 with
  every convenience of the 20th century. Its beautiful decor
  include crystal chandeliers, parquet floors, a grand piano
  and a graceful staircase connecting the two reception floors
The townhouse accommodates up to 125 guests for cocktail parties
  and wedding receptions and 75 for buffet dinners. The house is
  also well suited to corporate functions and business meetings

Murray Hill Townhouse

A Private Club Overlooking a Private Park
New York, N.Y.

737-7536

Built before the Civil War and "Victorianized" by architect
  Calvert Vaux, this designated National Historic Landmark
  and former residence of Governor Samuel Tilden, offers
  high ceilinged rooms enhanced by stained glass designed
  by John LaFarge. Glass and woodcarved ceilings including
  a unique and priceless stained glass structure called "The
  Domed," designed by 19th century glass master Donald MacDonald.
Guest capacity: 200 sitdown in Main Gallery
Available primarily on weekends
Caterer on premises

Racquet Club in Yorkville
New York, N.Y.

737-7536

5 floor facility with 14 squash courts, restaurant, bar, party room
Seating capacity: 50 in 2nd floor restaurant and bar, 150 standup
  in 3rd floor party room with bar
Rental fee: negotiable; approximately $100 to non-members
  for party room
3rd floor party room surrounded by plants and glass. Looks
  out onto exhibition court
Food may be served by space's restaurant or by caterer of your
  choice. Alcohol must be served by premises' restaurant
Suggested uses: meeting, party

Red Brick Federal Style Townhouse 737-7536
New York, N.Y.

Built in 1846, this historic Village landmark features a
   contemporary, multi-level home-like interior
Guest capacity: up to 75 persons
Caterer available or bring your own

"The Room" on West 13th Street 737-7536
New York, N.Y.

A newly created dining/meeting room area with easy street access
Seating capacity: 200 for cocktails; 100 for buffet or sitdown dining
Flexible stage area, reception bar, controlled lighting; food may
   be served only by caterer on premises
Suggested uses: dance, lecture, presentation, etc.

"The Room" on West 13th Street

Streamlined Railroad Diners 737-7536

Dining room car No. 406, built for the New York Central in 1947,
   and kitchen-bar car No. 1572, built in 1950 for the Santa Fe
   were formerly operated on such famous trains as the
   "Twentieth Century Limited" and "Santa Fe Chief." The
   diners feature fine views of the Hudson River and midtown
   skyline. Now parked on West 30th Street and adjacent to the
   new Convention Center, there is a 200 ft. long station platform
   for cocktails or dancing. Parking for 75 cars at the door.
Up to 100 guests for buffet or cocktail entertaining, 64 for
   sit-down dining

Streamlined Railroad Diners

Studio Loft With Roof Terrace
New York, N.Y.

737-7536

Situated on 2nd floor of a two-story building, this white-walled rectangular photographer's studio on East 34th Street has access to roof for roof terrace parties

Guest capacity: 300 maximum for cocktails; 75 for sitdown dinners

Special feature: contemporary, fully-appointed kitchen for instructional or advertising purposes

Studio Loft With Roof Terrace

A Uniquely Private Setting

737-7536

Built in 1832, this renovated historic Village townhouse, with its sleek modern duplex and garden, lends unpretentious elegance to very special events. A beautifully appointed open kitchen and dining room occupy the garden level while reception area and lounge, complete with stainless steel working fireplace, occupy the floor above.

40 to 80 for cocktail parties; 30 to 65 for omelet parties and buffets; 20 for sit-down dining

Resident chef on premises

A Uniquely Private Setting

For additional PRIVATE PARTIES/PRIVATE PLACES listings call (212) 737-7536

Also see: BOATS
DISCOS
HOTELS
LOFTS
PRIVATE PARTIES/PRIVATE PLACES (near New York City)
PRIVATE PARTIES/PUBLIC PLACES (in New York City)
PRIVATE PARTIES/PUBLIC PLACES (near New York City)
RINKS

* * * * * * *

Hilltop Hudson Valley Mansion

PRIVATE PARTY/ PRIVATE PLACES

(near New York City)

Hilltop Hudson Valley Mansion (212) 737-7536
Dobbs Ferry, N.Y.

Built in 1894 by J.J. McComb who made his fortune from the invention of the cotton tie. This mansion was described as "the handsomest house on the Hudson River."

The main features of the house are a two-story great central hall with all rooms on the ground floor opening onto it and a 38' x 38' octagonal library with painted skylight. Parquet floors. On one side of the hall is a large marble double staircase, on the other is an elaborate open fireplace twelve feet wide. Baby grand piano.

Guest capacity: up to 200 sitdown; additional guests may be accommodated on outside grounds and porch

Food may be served by caterer of your choice

Particularly suitable for weddings and large parties

English Country Estate/Conference Center

English Country Estate/Conference Center (212) 737-7536

This 28-room stone manor house with slate roof and leaded windows features walled gardens, solar-heated pool, 5 fireplaces, four-poster and canopy beds, and fine food. Vacant for thirty years, it was completely restored in 1979. Its adjacent farmhouse, *The Century*, built in 1734 was restored in 1980.

Located in Dutchess County, two hours from New York City, it is favored by leading corporations for think-tanks and meetings.

17 individual or 15 double occupancies.

The House on Library Plaza
New Rochelle, N.Y.

(212) 737-7536

This late 19th century neo-Italianate Renaissance two story
   structure with 12 foot ceilings serves as an interesting
   background for its new owner, a food researcher, whose
   complete restoration is with public access in mind. Located
   on red brick Library Plaza, facility is 32 minutes from New York City.
Guest capacity: 100 upstairs
   40 downstairs
   14 seated at dining room table
Professional kitchen and kitchen garden, closed circuit TV,
   ample parking; outside caterers welcome.
Suggested uses: TV commercial, food photography, taste testing,
   private dinner

Spacious Private School Near New York City
Dobbs Ferry, N.Y.

(212) 737-7536

Modern dining room/ballroom with picture windows
   looking out onto 60 acres of woods, jogging trails and
   30 acres of landscaped grounds
Guest capacity: 600 sitdown with room for dancing/
   1000 for cocktails
Note: School is also available as a conference site or special
   center for gifted children, etc., in summer. Dormitory
   accommodations are for 200.

Victorian Mansion/Now Private School

Victorian Mansion/Now Private School
Bernardsville, New Jersey

(212) 737-7536

Built in 1894 by George Post, this Victorian structure,
   surrounded by 40 acres of landscaped grounds, was the
   home of John Dryden, founder of the Prudential Life
   Insurance Company.
This elaborate property, which is now a private school, makes
   seven rooms available for private parties: the tapestry room,
   the main dining room, 2 sitting rooms, the library, the
   solarium with fountain and the large drawing room with fireplace.
Guest capacity: 200 maximum
Available evenings and weekends
Baby grand piano; food may be served only by space's own caterer
Suggested uses: reception, corporate party, family gathering, wedding

A White-washed Room in a Water Mill
Clinton, New Jersey

(212) 737-7536

A four-story water tower serves as museum depicting
   19th century American life.
Guest capacity: under 100 sitdown
                additional capacity on grounds outdoors
Bring caterer of your choice

****

The Dairy

PRIVATE PARTY/ PUBLIC PLACES

(in New York City)

American Museum of Natural History 873-6380
Central Park West at 79th Street
New York, N.Y. 10024
Contact: Marilyn Badaracco

Private Museum Viewing/Reception

Private receptions and dinners under a 94' blue whale,
  preceded by private viewings of selected exhibitions.
Guest capacity: 200 minimum for reception
                300 minimum for sitdown dinner in Hall of Ocean Life
Rental fee: corporate contribution
Suitable for corporations and conventions. Not available for fund-
  raising purposes.
Caterer on premises

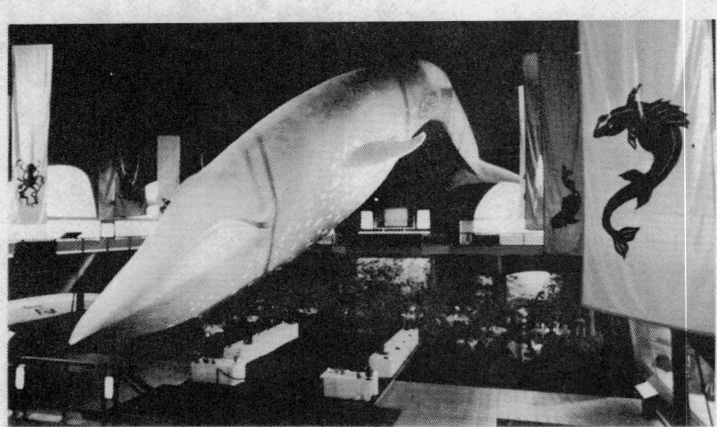

American Museum of Natural History

America's Only Automat 737-7536
(on Manhattan's East Side)
New York, N.Y.

Conceived in 1911 and recently refurbished in art deco style
  with etched glass and mirrored columns, its unique
  little Automat windows can serve up any food desired.
Guest capacity: 250 sitdown; 400 buffet-style
Suggested uses: all manner of special events are possible
  including a dance, roller disco or a theme party

America's Only Automat

Avery Fisher Hall 580-8700
Lincoln Center for the Performing Arts
Lincoln Center Plaza
65th Street & Broadway
New York, N.Y. 10023
Contact: Delmar Hendricks, Booking Manager

Grand Promenade and lobbies
Guest capacity: 1200 cocktails, Grand Promenade; 100 Choral Room
Available to both private and corporate persons depending on performance schedule
Caterer on premises

Blackwell House 832-4562
500 Main Street
Roosevelt Island, N.Y. 10044
Contact: Mrs. Shirley Margolin

In the 17th century Roosevelt Island, then called East River Island, together with Queens and Manhattan was granted to John Manning by his friend, the Duke of York. John Manning, however, surrendered New York to the Dutch in 1673 and was exiled on East River Island for this deed. Upon Mr. Manning's step-daughter's marriage to Robert Blackwell, the Blackwell family became identified with this island for 150 years. In 1828, the City of New York bought the island from the Blackwell's and began using it as a site for hospitals and prisons.
Blackwell House, which was restored in 1975, offers a unique panoramic view of New York City. Available for meetings primarily by community groups and, on occasion, for rent to corporate and business groups, etc.
Guest capacity: 25/30
Note: Access to the island is via the 60th Street tramway or by car or limousine across the Queensborough Bridge

Brooklyn Botanic Garden 737-7536
Brooklyn, N.Y.

Auditorium, rotunda, dining room, outdoors
Seating capacity: 150 sit-down in rotunda; 60 sit-down in dining room; 50 acres of grounds
Stage, platform, pianos, limited kitchen facilities; food may be served by caterer of your choice
Suggested uses: organizational and corporate meeting, reception, wedding, etc.
Note: Rental is subject to approval. Outdoor areas available Mondays and after 6:00 p.m. other days

Brooklyn Botanic Garden

The Dairy 360-8236
The Central Park Conservancy
830 Fifth Avenue
New York, N.Y. 10021

Recently restored to its 1870 Victorian Gothic charm, this delightful structure was originally designed by the architect Calvert Vaux, associate to landscape architect Frederick Law Olmsted, the creator of Central Park. Presently serving as the Visitor Information Center and located near "the Zoo and the Carousel," the Dairy's pastoral setting is a rare juxtaposition of repose and innocence in the middle of Manhattan.
Its 59' x 21' Great Hall and 20' high ceiling, offer excellent acoustics. The decorative Loggia overlooking the ice skating rink adds a roofed outdoor space.
Guest capacity: 100 sitdown*
30 in adjacent theater
*additional guests may be accommodated in Loggia
Available for special functions all day and evening on Mondays as well as after 4:30 p.m. Tuesday through Sunday
Food may be served by caterer of your choice

An 18th Century Stone Coach House/Stable, Now Museum 737-7536
New York, N.Y.

This elegant Federal building, completed in 1799, is situated on land once owned by Colonel William Stephens Smith and Abigail Adams Smith, daughter of President John Adams.

Located in what now is New York's upper Eastside, the coach house/stable had been converted into a residence and a hotel which featured "fresh water bathing in the East River." The handsome cut-stone house surrounded by an 18th century-style garden, is now owned and maintained by the Colonial Dames of America as a museum

Guest capacity: 200 for lectures; 150 sitdown dinners; 75/100 dinner dance in auditorium which is adjacent to the Museum

Galley kitchen. Bring your own caterer. Tour of Museum and garden may be included in special function

Note: Available for rental to non-profit groups only

An 18th Century Stone Coach House/Stable, Now Museum

Grand Central Station 340-2135
Consolidated Rail Corporation
466 Lexington Avenue
New York, N.Y. 10017
Contact: R.J. Tracy, Manager, Real Estate

North Balcony, Main Level, Waiting Room, Lower Level

Guest capacity: 300 North Balcony, overlooks Main Level and Information Booth; several thousand persons for Main Level and Lower Level. Capacity depends on use

Suggested uses: major fund-raising events, promotions, press parties, etc. Food may be served by caterer of your choice

Grand Central Station

Former Greenhouse/Now Restaurant   737-7536
(view of Palisades and Hudson River)
New York, N.Y.

Penthouse restaurant with terrace atop a Columbia University building
Guest capacity: 200; 150 in Terrace Room and on terrace; 50/60
    in Greenhouse Dining Room
Suggested uses: all private parties, especially a wedding

Former Union Hall and Neighborhood Bar/Now Irish Pub   737-7536
New York, N.Y.

Located in a typical 100-year-old Yorkville brownstone, this
    completely restored facility offers a private bar and wood-
    panelled dining/tap room upstairs plus fireplace
Guest capacity: 75 sitdown/50 with dancing. Both floors of this
    establishment may be made available on occasion, thus
    doubling guest capacity
Suggested uses: brunch, retirement party, alumni reunion, graduation
    party, christening, organizational dinner meeting, wedding

Hayden Planetarium   873-1300
Central Park West and 81st Street
New York, N.Y. 10024
Contact: Gwendolyn Gwyn, Public Relations

Guest capacity: 660 in Sky Theater; 700 buffet/300 to 350
    sitdown dinner
Rental fee: by corporate contribution
Caterer on premises
Suggested uses: corporate evenings offer special Museum Sky Show
    as well as cocktails and dinner

International Tavern Hospitality Suite   621-8295
Schenley Distillers Company   621-8297
888 Seventh Avenue (38th floor)
New York, N.Y. 10019
Contact: Lester Dember, Public Relations

Lounge with bar
Seating capacity: 75 for cocktails
Rental fee: none
View of the Hudson River
Note: Space is only available to non-profit groups from 5 p.m. to
    7 p.m. Public service oriented groups are particularly welcome

Kingsland Homestead   939-0647
143-35 37th Avenue (at Parson's Boulevard)
Flushing, Queens 11354
Contact: Secretary

Seating capacity: approximately 45 in meeting room
Food may be served by caterer of your choice
Suggested use: party
Note: Smoking is not allowed. Space has limited availability

Library and Museum of the Performing Arts 737-7536
Main Gallery
111 Amsterdam Avenue at 65th Street
New York, N.Y.

Guest capacity: 500 sitdown dinner/1000 for cocktails
Rental fee: varies
Dance floor; food may be served by caterer of your choice
Note: Use of the Main Gallery is restricted to members connected
   to the performing arts and depends on exhibit schedule

Metropolitan Museum of Art TR 9-5500
Fifth Avenue & 82nd Street ext. 3773
New York, N.Y. 10028
Contact: Mr. Chris Giftos, Coordinator for Social Events

The museum is available to corporate sponsors of the museum
   and/or its events

Metropolitan Opera Association 799-3100
Lincoln Center for the Performing Arts
Lincoln Center Plaza
Broadway & 63rd Street
New York, N.Y. 10023
Contact: Al Hoebrecht, Manager, Grand Tier Restaurant

Guest capacity: 150 and up sitdown dinner/400 and up stand-up
   in Grand Tier Restaurant
Suggested uses: Private party may be combined with opera performance

Morris-Jumel Mansion

Morris-Jumel Mansion 923-8008
West 160th Street & Edgecombe Avenue
New York, N.Y. 10032
Contact: Audrey Braver, Museum Director

Built as a summer house in 1765 by Colonel Roger Morris,
a retired British officer, it is Manhattan's oldest residence.
Aaron Burr, third Vice-President of the United States,
was married in the front parlor. The house was bought
in 1903 by the City of New York and opened as an
historic house and museum in 1907 under the auspices
of the Washington Headquarters Association
Seating capacity: 20/50
Outdoor garden; food may be served by caterer on premises
or by caterer of your choice
Suggested uses: luncheon, seminar, benefit, location shooting

Museum of Holography   737-7536
(in SoHo)
New York, N.Y.

Auditorium, exhibit/reception area
Seating capacity: 50 in auditorium; 150 in exhibit space
Rental fee: $500 minimum
Kitchen; food may be served by caterer of your choice
Suggested uses: museum dinner party with futuristic atmosphere
due to surrounding holograms which are three-dimensional,
in-motion laser beam photo images

Note: Preferred private party availability is on Monday and
Tuesday evenings. Not available during daytime hours

Museum of Holography

The New York Botanical Garden   220-8774
Enid A. Haupt Conservatory
Bronx, N.Y. 10458
Contact: Eileen Barrett, Director of Special Events

A series of 11 magnificent greenhouses, or "plant galleries," including
a central palm court with a 90-foot dome
Guest capacity: 50/1000
The Conservatory is available to corporate sponsors of the Garden
and/or its events
Note: Fund-raising, weddings or similar events are not allowed

New York Botanical Garden
Snuff Mill Restaurant
Bronx, N.Y. 10458
Contact: Jennie Colucci, Secretary to the Personnel Manager
  or Eric Friberg, Caterer

220-8762
(Secretary)
547-0511
(Caterer)

Room, terrace, garden
Seating capacity: 150
Overlooks the Bronx River
Suggested use: wedding
Note: Facility used to be an 18th century snuff mill
  and is an historic landmark

New York Botanical Garden/Enid A. Haupt Conservatory

New York Chamber of Commerce & Industry
Great Hall and Dining Room
65 Liberty Street
New York, N.Y. 10005
Contact: Evelyn Ortner

561-2020

Guest capacity: 200 sitdown dinner in Great Hall, 300 for cocktails;
  195 in Dining Room, 300 for cocktails
Rental fee: varies
Food may be served by caterer of your choice
Note: Available only to corporate, non-profit or government groups

New York Chamber of Commerce & Industry

New York Experience Theater 737-7536
Rockefeller Center
New York, N.Y.

A motion picture theater showing the multisensory "New York
  Experience" film, an exhibit recreating New York City at
  the turn of the century, and an antique amusement arcade
  make a private party package
Seating capacity: 350 guests may be accommodated
Complete audio-visual equipment, quadrophonic sound system,
  45 motion picture and slide projectors; caterer on premises
  or bring your own
Suggested uses: convention, banquet, cocktail, buffet, press conference,
  sales seminar, fund-raiser, private party

New York Experience Theater

New York Exposition and Convention Center 930-0303
(Between 11th and 12th Avenues and 34th-39th Streets)
New York, N.Y. 10001
Contact: Convention Center Development Corporation,
  Public Relations Department

Exhibition space
Seating capacity: 140,000 sq. ft. of space available for 35,000
  people in meeting and special events rooms; total floor area is
  1.8 million sq. ft. (500,000 sq. ft. on Upper Level, 250,000 sq. ft.
  on Lower Level); 1 acre outdoor plaza, on-site kitchens
This will be the largest exhibition space ever contained within
  a single building. Panoramic view of waterfront.
Note: The architects are I.M. Pei & Partners Lewis, Turner
  Partnership. Opening date of this $375,000,000 center is Spring 1984.

New York Public Library 737-7536
Fifth Avenue & 42nd Street
New York, N.Y.

Astor Hall is located on the first floor of the Fifth Avenue side of the Library
Guest capacity: 1000 for cocktails

Rotunda is located on the third floor
Guest capacity: 300 for a stand-up reception

Trustee Room is located on the second floor
Guest capacity: 200 for cocktails

Room 207
Guest capacity: 30 conference-style

Rental fee: upon request. Special rates to corporate contributors

Note: Facilities are open to the public, but rentee must meet with the approval of the Trustees of the Library

New York Public Library

New York Public Transit Exhibit 330-3060
Boerum Place & Schermerhorn Street
Brooklyn, N.Y. 11201
Contact: Aubrey Surgeon, Public Relations Department

Transit exhibit is located in an unused subway station with a 600 ft. mezzanine with space for special events and a platform lined with vintage cars

Suggested uses: all special events are possible including a ride on one of the vintage subway trains and a dance

Nostalgia Special

Nostalgia Special
New York Transit Authority
370 Jay Street
Brooklyn, N.Y. 11201
Contact: Dennis J. Wendling, Manager of Special Events
  or Aubrey Surgeon for Public Transit Exhibit

330-3164
(Wendling)
330-3060 or 360-3063
(Surgeon)

Vintage subway cars in mint condition available for private
  party charter. Guests may embark at the IND line station at
  57th Street and Avenue of the Americas in Manhattan, or at
  any other IND line station and begin party in transit. Vintage
  cars can be outfitted like parlor cars with tables, etc., food and
  drink may be served aboard. Train may be directed to travel to
  the New York Public Transit Exhibit in Brooklyn for a sumptuous
  buffet or dinner dance amidst period subway cars.
Transit exhibit is located in an unused subway station with a 600 ft. mezzanine

Old Merchant's House
29 East 4th Street
New York, N.Y.
Contact: Carol Roberto

777-1089

The only 19th century house in Manhattan which has survived
  intact with its original furniture and family memorabilia.
  Its family room and kitchen on ground floor are occasionally
  available for private functions by appointment
Guest capacity: 12 sitdown; 45 for cocktails
Small garden

Old Merchant's House

Phillips Fine Art Auctioneers
867 Madison Avenue (at 72nd Street)
New York, N.Y. 10021
Contact: Cintra Huber, Director of Public Relations & Advertising

570-4841

This world-renowned fine art auction house will occasionally
  make available three of its rooms for special events
Second Floor Guest Capacity: 200 in Auction Room; 100 in Exhibit Room
Third Floor Guest Capacity: 100 in Ballroom
The Rhinelander Mansion, in which this auction house is situated,
  is a five-story building modeled after a 16th century French chateau
  and built in 1895. It is one of New York's great "Gilded Age" mansions

Suggested uses: benefits and receptions of a cultural nature. Events
  may be coordinated with special sales/exhibits sponsored by the
  auction house, i.e., U.S. and foreign stamps, American furniture
  and decoration, art nouveau and art deco, etc.
Note: Buffet and tray snacks only are allowed

Phillips Fine Art Auctioneers

A Private Floor With Entertainment 737-7536
(Carnegie Hall and Central Park)
New York, N.Y.

Under 100 guests may have a cabaret floor and show of their own.
  Light supper or buffet
Suggested uses: surprise birthday party, retirement party,
  business entertaining, etc.
On Monday and Tuesday evenings another private floor (without
  entertainment) is available. European country decor. It is
  especially suitable for an organizational dinner meeting

Queens Botanical Garden 737-7536
Flushing, N.Y.

Auditorium, wedding garden
Seating capacity: 120 buffet/70 lecture-hall style/50 for sitdown
  dining in auditorium; 200 stand-up/150 auditorium-style
  in Wedding Garden
Rental fee: $250 minimum for up to 4 hours, $75 for each
  additional hour in the auditorium; $100 for the first 25 people
  for 1 hour, $1 for each additional person per hour in Wedding Garden
Sound system (available for music by special arrangement), kitchen
  (for serving only); food may be served by caterer of your choice
Suggested uses: reception, photography, party, wedding

Radio City Music Hall 246-0945
1260 Avenue of the Americas
New York, N.Y. 10020
Contact: Sales Department

Elegantly restored American landmark; guests can be accommodated
   in Art Deco Grand Lounge, Grand Foyer or First Mezzanine
Guest capacity: 200/800 in Grand Lounge; 300/800 in Grand Foyer;
   300 in First Mezzanine for dinner-dance, banquet, cocktail
   reception (capacity depends on use)
Rental fee: upon request
Caterers, florists, orchestras can be recommended
Available to both private and corporate parties
Suggested uses: cocktail receptions, benefit dinner-dances or concerts,
   fashion shows, press parties; also Group Rate tickets to Radio City
   Music Hall stage show in combination with cocktail reception
   or dinner

Restored Village 737-7536
Staten Island, N.Y.

Auditorium, exhibit space, historic buildings, pond
Seating capacity: 125 in auditorium in old Court House;
   10 acres of space are available
Rental fee: varies with number of people and location
Platform, winding staircase, kitchen; food may be served
Suggested uses: exhibit, lecture, meeting, outdoor performance,
   promotion, wedding
Note: Space is only available upon approval of the Board of Directors
   and there are limitations due to the historic nature of the premises

Restored Village

Snug Harbor Cultural Center 448-2500
914 Richmond Terrace
Staten Island, N.Y. 10301
Contact: Tara Ryan, Program Coordinator

Space is an 80-acre national historic landmark site in a park setting.
   Opened in 1831 as a sailors' retirement home, it now is a non-profit
   cultural and educational organization which serves as home for
   independent visual and performing arts groups
Proscenium theatre, rehearsal space, classroom, conference room,
   exhibit space, reception area, large recreation hall, community gallery

Governor's house is a Victorian mansion consisting of porch, two front parlors, dining room and downstairs kitchen
Seating capacity: 700 in theatre; 200 in next largest space; 30/65 in Governor's House
Rental fee: negotiable, $25 for 4 hours in meeting room; $100 for 4 hours in recreation hall; $300 for day use of community gallery (when available); $100 for Governor's House; $50 minimum for scenic grounds
Platform, piano, fireplace, dance floor, restaurant; kitchen's food may be served by caterer of your choice
View of New York Harbor
Suggested uses: all community or arts related activities are possible as well as weddings

South Street Seaport Museum 766-9020
East River and Fulton Street
New York, N.Y. 10038
Contact: David Beggs

Historic ships berthed at Piers 15 and 16.

Also see: BOATS
PIERS

The United Nations 754-6206
Delegates Dining Room
First Avenue & 44th Street
New York, N.Y. 10017
Contact: Michael Hanlon, Liaison Officer

Facility overlooks East River and is open to the public. If event is in afternoon, it can be combined with a tour of the United Nations
Guest capacity: 500 for lunch/350 for dinner/500 to 800 for cocktails

U.S. Custom House

U.S. Custom House
Bowling Green
New York, N.Y.

264-2600

The rehabilitation of public spaces belonging to this grande dame of Beaux Arts should be completed by 1984. By then the tar that has covered its rotunda's skylight since World War II will have been removed; its courtyard will be paved with stone and covered with a two-story-high glass roof; the boiler room will have been transformed into an auditorium, etc.

Wave Hill Center for Environmental Studies

Wave Hill Center for Environmental Studies
675 West 252nd Street
Bronx, N.Y.

737-7536

Built in the early 19th century as a family estate for William Lewis Morris and lived in by publisher William Appleton, writer Mark Twain and others, Wave Hill was a gathering place for thinkers and notables. Overlooking the Hudson and the Palisades, this 150-year-old New York City property was later founded as an arboretum and botanic garden. Its mansion is a two-story fieldstone house designed in the Greek Revival style, with Armor Hall providing an excellent setting for indoor functions

Auditorium/ballroom/concert hall, 3 conference rooms, patio, garden, exhibit space, reception areas, dining room

Platform, piano, dance floor; kitchen; food may be served by caterer of your choice

Suggested uses: outdoor and indoor motion picture shooting and fashion photography, guided tours

Note: Space is available to non-profit groups and corporate members for a meeting, conference, lecture, etc., on weekdays; weekends after 4:30 p.m. For special functions, the facility is available on a one-time per year basis to corporate and profit making groups upon payment of a corporate membership contribution. Individual private events such as weddings are not allowed

* * * * * * *

The Casino, Saratoga Springs, N.Y.

PRIVATE PARTY/ PUBLIC PLACES

(near New York City)

Banquet Facility (212) 737-7536
Yonkers, N.Y.

Estate spanning 5 acres; country club atmosphere
Guest capacity: 20/500
Dance floor, terrace, lawn, parking on premises; food served
　by resident caterer
Suggested uses: banquet, reception, shower, anniversary,
　engagement, wedding

Bedford Hills Community House (914) 666-2803
Main & Church Streets
Bedford Hills, N.Y. 10507
Contact: Mrs. Gustin, Rental Agent

Auditorium/exhibit space, lounge, meeting rooms, patio
Seating capacity: 200 in auditorium; 40/60 in meeting rooms
Space was built as a war memorial and has French doors leading
　from the auditorium to the patio
Stage, piano, kitchen; food may be served by caterer of your choice
Suggested uses: dinner, meeting, class, dance, wedding

The Casino (212) 737-7536
Saratoga Springs, New York

This large red brick Victorian structure served the Saratoga
　mineral spa and horse racing society as an elegant gambling
　casino since 1870. The great Dining Hall, designed by
　Clarence Luce, was added in 1903. Its ceiling is honeycombed
　with stained glass windows giving this room an extraordinary
　grandeur of magnificent diffused light
Guest capacity: 325 for sitdown dinner in Dining Hall
Completely restored, the Dining Hall now rents out for
　private functions including a reception, benefit or wedding

1828 Quaker Meeting House (914) 723-1744
937 White Plains Post Road
Scarsdale, N.Y. 10583
Contact: Marcia Atkins

Conference room, meeting room
Seating capacity: 12 in conference room; 23' x 23' of space
　is available in the meeting room
Rental fee: by contribution
Note: Smoking is not allowed
Mailing address is: The Scarsdale Historical Society
　　　　　　　　　937 White Plains Post Road
　　　　　　　　　Scarsdale, N.Y. 10583

1828 Quaker Meeting House

Hudson Valley Wine Co., Inc. (914) 691-7296
Blue Point Road (212) 594-5394
Highland, N.Y. 12528
Contact: Kathleen Welch, Reservations

Established in 1907, this 325 acre winery estate, which is a 1½ hour
 drive from New York City offers vineyards, stone buildings,
 and more than a mile of scenic Hudson riverfront

Guest capacity: 15/100 sitdown in Manor House; 300 outdoors
 for a company picnic, etc.

Exclusive use of grounds and Manor House for an afternoon
 or evening event may be arranged for occasionally

Wine tours and tastings, picnic tables and tents for wedding
 parties are available

Suggested uses: organizational outing, company picnic, hayride,
 festival, apple picking, wedding

Hudson Valley Wine Co., Inc.

Lyndhurst (914) 631-0046
635 South Broadway
Tarrytown, N.Y. 10591
Contact: Nancy Richards, Assistant Administrator and Curator

Built in 1838 for William Paulding, a former Mayor of New York City,
 this Gothic Revival mansion was last privately owned by
 railroad magnate Jay Gould. Presently, it is one of ten historical
 museums owned and maintained by the National Trust for Historic
 Preservation in the United States

Fund-raising events for non-profit institutions or corporate
 members and major donors of the National Trust will be
 considered on an individual basis. Although the mansion,
 staffed by Lyndhurst guides, will be open to the party, food
 and drink will have to be consumed in tents on the lawn, with
 some activity permitted on the long veranda facing the Hudson
 River. Location shooting for commercial photography indoors
 and outdoors is allowed. Motion picture production, however,
 will most likely be confined to the outdoors. Grounds are
 available for picnics with admission charge. Purely private
 parties such as wedding receptions are not allowed.

Lyndhurst

Museum with Japanese Stroll Gardens
North Salem, N.Y.

(212) 737-7536

Fifty miles from New York City, the Hammond Museum stands
 on a hilltop commanding a view of rolling farmlands, lakes and woods

Guild Hall, though recently built, is a replica of a Medieval hall with
 fireplace and tapestries

Guest capacity: 100 for sit-down dinner in Guild Hall
                  100 for luncheon in outdoor courtyard

Terrazzo dance floor in Guild Hall, stage

Museum has its own catering service. If outside catering is brought in,
 museum staff must be hired for serving, etc.

Suggested uses: lecture, corporate dinner or luncheon, music recital,
 film showing, wedding, etc.

Museum on the Hudson River
Yonkers, New York

(212) 737-7536

Set in Trevor Park overlooking the Hudson, this unique museum complex consists of Glenview, a Victorian mansion, the Contemporary Gallery which is an award-winning modern structure built into a slope on three levels, the Andrus Space Transit Planetarium, and the Courtyard or Sculpture Garden, situated in-between the Mansion and the Contemporary Gallery which serves beautifully for spring and fall music and dance performances. Films in the Planetarium may also serve as an adjunct.

Built in 1875 by John B. Trevor, the Victorian/Eastlake style mansion offers three fully restored rooms overlooking the Hudson and a Grand Hallway.

Guest capacity: 50 sitdown in Glenview mansion; 350 sitdown/ 800 cocktails in the Contemporary Gallery; 135 sitdown in Planetarium.

Food may be served by caterer of your choice. Fully equipped kitchen.

Note: Groups related to the Museum's activities in art, science and history are particularly welcome. For non-profit groups, the Museum is available on a cost cover basis; however, fundraising is not allowed. For corporate and profit-making groups, the facility is available on a one-time per year basis upon payment of a $2,000 corporate contribution plus all costs. Individual private events such as weddings are not allowed.

Museum on the Hudson River

North Shore Gold Coast Mansion
Glen Cove, N.Y.

(212) 737-7536

This handsomely landscaped Georgian Mansion bordering
   Long Island Sound, which presently serves as a nature
   preserve and conference center, was built in the early 1900's
   by the sons of the oil magnate and philanthropist Charles M. Pratt.
10 stately rooms, English-style formal garden, 200 acres of quiet
   forest and landscaped vistas
Guest capacity: approximately 200 sitdown
Rental fee: approximately $250 to $600 and up depending on
   room used
Food may be served by caterer of your choice subject to
   management approval
Suggested uses: meeting, conference, educational seminar. Wedding
   for Nassau residents only

North Shore Gold Coast Mansion

Wainwright House
260 Stuyvesant Avenue
Rye, N.Y.

(212) 737-7536

Auditorium, meeting room, 3 conference/meeting rooms
Seating capacity: 125 in 20' x 50' auditorium; 40 persons
   theatre style in each 18' x 28' meeting room
Piano, fireplace, winding staircase, kitchen; food may be served
Space was formerly a private home modeled after a French chateau
   with view of an inlet from Long Island Sound
Suggested uses: concert, class, exhibit, lecture, meeting

Wainwright House

Wayside Cottage
Scarsdale, N.Y.
(212) 737-7536

This historical landmark was built in 1725. Listed in the National Register of Historic Places. It is owned by the Village of Scarsdale and is maintained and run by the Junior League of Scarsdale.

Seating capacity: 100 in largest room; 35 in smaller room

Large flagstone patio extending from largest room; a tent may be erected

Food may be served by caterer of your choice

Available for a variety of social functions; parties, seminars, meetings, etc.

Tables, chairs, dishes are included in modest rental fee

Wayside Cottage

* * * * * * *

CHILDREN'S BIRTHDAY PARTIES

CAROUSELS

Central Park Manhattan	744-9779
Coney Island Brooklyn	372-0275
Prospect Park Brooklyn	965-6586
Forest Park Queens	846-9228
Flushing Meadow-Corona Park Queens	373-0121

Carousel, Central Park Photo credit: New York City Department of Parks & Recreation

Birthday Room
(Upper East Side)
New York, N.Y.

737-7536

A cozy room with working fireplace and brick walls. Children
 ages 3 and up celebrate their own birthday party with careful
 supervision by the staff.
Guest capacity: 24 children with several adults for a birthday
 party; 12/15 for a meeting.
An oven is available so all can participate in baking the cake.
 Sound system, festive lighting, carpeting. All manner of
 theme parties are possible. Staff coordinates entire party.
Note: An indoor skating studio is nearby which can accommodate
 25 children. $150 an hour includes skate rental and instructor.

Mostly Magic (Nightclub/Theater)
55 Carmine Street
New York, N.Y. 10014

924-1472

A magician or clown experienced in performing for children,
 plus an inscribed birthday cake, beverages and party favors
 are provided on Saturdays at 1:00 and at 3:00;
 Sundays at 2:00
Rental fee: $200 for 25 children
Note: At least one adult guardian must be in attendance

Museum of the City of New York
103rd Street and Fifth Avenue
New York, N.Y. 10029
Contact: Barbara Davy, Education Department

534-1672
ext. 206

Birthday parties for children from 6 to 12 years of age are offered
 from Tuesday through Friday from 3:00 to 4:30 p.m. Includes
 a partial tour of museum, visit to a 17th century Dutch room with
 lecture on life in New Amsterdam with a "please touch" policy,
 cake, ice cream, games, prizes and souvenirs. A minimum of 10 and
 a maximum of 15 children can be accommodated at $12 per child

Rumpelmayer's Restaurant
St. Moritz Hotel
50 Central Park South
New York, N.Y. 10019
Contact: Lido Santos, Food & Beverages

755-5800
(Santos)
246-0520
(Hansom Cabs)

Children's birthday parties consisting of birthday cake, punch,
 small sandwiches, etc., may be held from 2:00 to 4:00 p.m. in
 any one of three private rooms adjacent to the restaurant. The
 party may be combined with a Central Park carriage ride. This
 arrangement must be made separately by calling Hansom Cabs
 Horse Drawn Carriages

Sutton Gym
22 East 38th Street (Lancaster Hotel)
New York, N.Y. 10016
Contact: Bill Hladik or John Szaraz

684-5833

Fully supervised hour-long exercise and gymnastic class
    and additional half hour use of space for refreshments
Ages: 3 years through teens
Rental fee: $7.50 per child. Minimum 10 children
Side horse, balance beam, low bars, parallel bars, rings,
    trapeze, tumbling mats, mini- and
    full-sized trampoline are on premises

Thirteenth Street Theatre   675-6677
50 West 13th Street
New York, N.Y. 10011
Contact: Edith O'Hara or Anthony Sorrero

Seating capacity: 75 in theatre; 30 in lobby
Bring your own birthday cake and refreshments to be served
    in lobby. See show either before, or after party. Special children's
    shows every Saturday and Sunday at 1:00 and 3:00 p.m. $10 for
    lobby plus $2.50 per person charge for show

The U.S.S. Ling   (201) 488-9770
Submarine Memorial Association
P.O. Box 395
Hackensack, N.J. 07602
Contact: Paula Leonardi

Birthday parties on a World War II submarine moored in Hackensack,
    New Jersey. Parties include a nautical birthday cake, a Captain's
    hat for the birthday child, a guided tour of the U.S.S. Ling,
    tablecloth, napkins, glasses, forks, candles and punch
Rental fee: $30 for six children plus $1.00 for each additional child,
    $2.00 for each adult and additional charge for cake if larger than
    7". $10 non-refundable advance deposit required
Note: Birthday parties are arranged for weekdays only

Also see: Goodskates

* * * * * * *

Capital Children's Museum   (202) 543-8600
(A Private Participatory Museum)
800 Third Street, N.E.
Washington, D.C. 20003
Contact: Adele Alexander

Formerly a convent, the Museum's rooms are available
    for special functions at all times when closed to the public.
    Its high-ceilinged former chapel now replicates a town plaza
    in Mexico, including a fountain church, cafe, etc. Premises
    are suitable for both children and adults.
Guest capacity: 500 maximum, plus additional warm-weather
    capacity in enclosed grounds
Rental fee: by contribution to the Museum

Capital Children's Museum

A Museum House (212) 737-7536
St. Louis, Missouri

A restored 1845 Federal row house and birthplace of
 children's poet Eugene Field is now a historic house and
 toy museum
Guest capacity: up to 150
Available for elegant private functions in the evenings and
 during the day on Sundays and Mondays. Also early Sunday brunch.

A Museum House

Film & Photography (only):

    French Country Loft 737-7536
    11th Street & University Place
    New York, N.Y.

This private art gallery has been lavishly decorated with
   French country and contemporary designer furniture
   to accompany an eclectic collection of contemporary
   art work
Gallery measures 55' x 100' and has 13' ceilings, arched windows,
   city views, open kitchen and is fully air-conditioned
Suitable for a location shooting, television cable, still
   photography, etc.

French Country Loft

Marion Castle (212) 737-7536
Stamford, Connecticut

Ballroom, formal garden, patio, pool
Many-turreted 29-room mansion was built for a movie
   entrepreneur in 1916 by the firm of Hunt and Hunt who
   designed the Metropolitan Museum of Art and the
   Vanderbilt Estate in Asheville, North Carolina. Present
   owners are stage costume designers and interior decorators
Suggested uses: location shooting

Marion Castle

Sniffen Court 683-5520
New York, N.Y. 10016
Contact: Peter Glen or Gary Stern

About the time of the Civil War, 8 buildings constructed
   in the early Romanesque revival style were used as stables
   by residents of Murray Hill. Now designated by the New York
   Landmarks Preservation Commission, the small, stone
   paved court creates a picturesque area in mid-Manhattan.
Available for film and photography only

A Victorian Vanderbilt Estate

PRIVATE PARTY PLACES (NATIONWIDE)

Villa Which Was Built For A Saloonkeeper (212) 737-7536
Little Rock, Arkansas

This Victorian home built in 1881 features tall arched windows, carved winged Gryphones and a spiral staircase. Its entire period-furnished downstairs is available for special functions

Guest capacity: 60 sitdown; 200 for cocktails plus 200 on the outdoor lawn

Food may be served by caterer of your choice

Villa Which Was Built For A Saloonkeeper

Napa Valley Winery (212) 737-7536
Rutherford, California

Founded by Gustave Niebaum in 1879, this winery, which is 1½ hours north of San Francisco, is a large native stone chateau, covered with Virginia Creeper which turns a reddish hue in the fall. On the second floor of the aging cellar, the cask-lined former fermentation room is available for private wine-related functions.

Guest capacity: 45 minimum/150 maximum. Outside caterers may be brought in. Caterer-in-Residence also available.

Suggested uses: Wine Tastings, luncheons, dinners for organizations, convention groups and consumer groups.

Napa Valley Winery

A Queen Anne Style Mansion
San Francisco, California

(212) 737-7536

The main floor can accommodate up to 150 for cocktails and hors d'oeuvres, 50 for a sitdown dinner

The lower level consists of a large wood paneled supper room which can accommodate 85 for a sitdown dinner; if more than 150 guests additional food and a bar on this level are arranged

Volunteers are available to circulate at parties in Victorian dress and to give informal house tours

Note: For lunches and brunches space is not available on Wednesdays or Sundays

A Queen Anne Style Mansion

Hampton Roads
A Presidential Railroad Car

737-7536

A private railroad car built in 1926 by the Pullman Company, reconverted into presidential car by Southern Railway in 1945. Fully air-conditioned

Accommodates 6 for luxurious overnight travel anywhere in the U.S., Canada and Mexico

Seating capacity: 20 maximum for one-day trips and 35 maximum when stationary in depot

Features: Two large staterooms, private baths with showers, full-size dining room seating 6-10 stainless steel kitchen, observation room seating 9, open rear canopied platform (for whistle stops) and presidential hopefuls

Meals: The *Hampton Roads* offers 24-hour complete gourmet meal service by professional chef. For one-day events catering may be arranged for locally.

Suggested uses: executive think-tanks en route to meetings, sport events, etc., family reunions, weddings/honeymoons, stars and superstars en route to performing engagements

Note: The car serves as the traveller's hotel when stops are made. Additional cars may be arranged for larger groups. Generally parked in Florida, *Hampton Roads* will travel anywhere in the U.S., Canada and Mexico.

Hampton Roads

Italian Renaissance Villa and Gardens
Miami, Florida

(212) 737-7536

In order to house his valuable antique art collection, James Dearing of the Harvester Corporation built this villa in the early twentieth century, carefully re-creating the details of Italian Renaissance villas

Italian Renaissance Villa and Gardens

Now run as a unique museum, the 69-room villa offers special
function spaces in: the Tea Room, in its courtyards, in its
marble-floored front entrance hall and on its Terrace called
The East Loggia, which faces Miami Bay.
Guest capacity: 400 sitdown on Terrace/East Loggia
150 buffet, indoors
Sub-tropical plants and foliage in formal Italian gardens.
Ocean breezes.
You may bring caterer of your choice.

Ship Museum

Ship Museum
Savannah, Georgia

(212) 737-7536

Museum is a four-storied, maritime museum on the Historic
Waterfront overlooking the Savannah River
Guest capacity: 300 guests maximum/75 for sitdown dinners
Top floor is carpeted with nautical decor; balcony overlooks
river. Dancing possible on 1st and 2nd floors
Food may be served by caterer of your choice
Suggested uses: meeting, reception, cocktail party

A Library/Cultural Center

A Library/Cultural Center
Chicago, Illinois

(212) 737-7536

The elaborate interior of Chicago's Library built in 1897
was renovated to serve also as a cultural center in 1977.
An architectural showcase of bronze, marble, mosaic and
stained glass, it offers spectacular public areas which are
suitable for concerts, receptions and cultural activities of all kinds

Guest capacity: up to 700 stand-up; 400 sitdown in Preston Bradley Hall; up to 350 stand-up in the Grand Army of the Republic Rotunda; up to 294 in Theater. The latter features a 20' x 24' proscenium stage, theatrical lighting and sound equipment along with sloped seating

Note: Use of the Cultural Center facilities is restricted to civic, educational or cultural non-profit organizations

An Urban Mansion With Windows Facing Inward

An Urban Mansion With Windows Facing Inward
Chicago, Illinois

(212) 737-7536

Built for a late 19th century industrialist, this famous example of architect Henry Hobson Richardson's work, who was a forerunner of Louis Sullivan and Frank Lloyd Wright, is now the home of the Chicago Architecture Foundation. Located near The Loop and McCormick Palace, its L-shaped design offers an inner courtyard with large windows facing onto it rather than onto the busy street. The landmark's fortress-like stone facade contradicts its inner warmth and privacy. Its balconied living hall, parlor and dining room are furnished with the warmly polished woods used by late 19th century American craftsmen who custom-designed the tables, desks, bookcases, etc.

Corporate Guest Capacity: 150 maximum; additional rooms available for smaller organizational meetings, use of outdoor courtyard

Food may be served by caterer of your choice

Note: Transportation in authentic 1890's horse-drawn carriages is available

An Old County Courthouse and Jail
Woodstock, Illinois

(212) 737-7536

Designed in 1857 by architect John Mills Van Osdel, now listed in the National Register of Historic Places, this three-story county courthouse still features its original impenetrable wooden doors, pressed tin ceilings, massive iron vaults, old record books, a winding stairway, and other vestiges of a time when Socialist leader Eugene V. Debs was jailed there during the Pullman strikes of the late 1800's, as well as bootleggers "Dapper Dan" McCarthy and bank robber Earl Weiss of the 1920's and 1930's.

Guest capacity: 2 in a solitary cell
12 in the Woodstock Room
200 in the Grand Courtroom atop the winding stairway
Caterer and restaurant on premises

An Old County Courthouse and Jail

The Mansion Which Was Built By A Wagon-Builder Named Studebaker
South Bend, Indiana

(212) 737-7536

Built in 1886 by Chicago architect Henry Ives Cobb, this fortress-like mansion of granite boulders features Romanesque arches and shuttered windows, a Medieval entranceway, a Grand Hall and stairway, variously shaped towers, colonetted verandas, 20 fireplaces and 40 rooms

Guest capacity: 300 sitdown in entire house
80 sitdown in Ballroom
Numerous additional smaller rooms

The mansion sits atop a ridge which commands a view of the St. Joseph River

Caterer on premises

The Mansion Which Was Built By A Wagon-Builder Named Studebaker   Photo credit: Jim Yoder

A Garden District Mansion
New Orleans, Louisiana

(212) 737-7536

A pre-Civil War mansion of Greek revival and Italianate
architecture with traditional second floor iron work
on the outside. Its ornate interior features gold leaf cornices,
Florentine mirrors, crystal chandeliers from one of the Royal
Imperial Palaces of St. Petersburg, stained glass windows and
a signed fresco by Tojetti on the ceiling of the Music Room.
Awning on the front veranda may be dropped for a quasi-
outdoor feeling. Members of the Women's Guild will act as
hostesses and, if desired, will wear the antebellum dresses
worn at the time the house was built

Guest capacity: 125 maximum for sitdown dinners; 250 maximum
for cocktails

A Garden District Mansion

The Plantation With 250 Year Old Oak Trees
Vacherie, Louisiana

(212) 737-7536

Sixty miles above New Orleans, a French sugar planter built
this plantation home in 1837/39 for his bride. Almost a
century later, this romantic home became one of the first
of the Great River Road plantations to be fully restored

Furnished just as its last owners had left it, house tours are
still conducted by their personal servants

Luncheon featuring local menus is served in an old slave quarter
building; the blacksmith's shed accommodates 150 for seated
meetings and two quarter houses are available for overnight
accommodations

The Plantation restaurant also caters outdoor picnics

Guest capacity: approximately 300 may be accommodated,
larger numbers by special arrangement

Suggested uses: corporate parties, weddings and honeymoons,
the estate is both a non-profit foundation and a National
Historic Landmark

The Plantation With 250 Year Old Oak Trees

The South's Largest Plantation House on the Banks of the Mississippi (212) 737-7536
Banks of the Mississippi
White Castle, Louisiana

With 53,000 sq. ft. under its original slate roof, this great home
 was built in 1859 in the style of a blend of Greek Revival
 and Italianate. Saved from total destruction during the Civil War
 through the kind act of a Northern gunboat officer who had been
 a former guest at the mansion, it is presently in mint condition
The White Ballroom, the most famous of its 64 rooms, can
 accommodate 200 for a wedding
Originally designed by renowned 19th century architect Henry
 Howard for John Hampdon Randolph, a wealthy sugar
 planter, this "American castle" offers great views of the
 Mississippi River, century-old live oaks, a pond and an island
 with Canadian geese and ducks.
Arrangements may be made for receptions, convention, weddings,
 and other functions. Overnight accommodations for up to
 14 guests with candlelight dinners and Planters Breakfasts,
 also available. Air-conditioned
Location: 2 hours north of New Orleans

The South's Largest Plantation House on the Banks of the Mississippi

The Mansion of the First Commander of the USS Enterprise (212) 737-7536
Riverdale, Maryland

The mansion which was constructed in 1939 for Captain
 Newton H. White, USN on a 500 acre estate in close
 proximity of Washington, D.C. is now available for private functions
Guest capacity: 200
Food may be served by caterer of your choice
Suggested uses: wedding and all manner of private functions

The Mansion of the First Commander of the USS Enterprise

Plaza Castle, A Former Armory Now Meeting & Exhibit Space (212) 737-7536
Boston, Massachusetts

Built in 1891 as an armory for the First Corps of Cadets
 and now a National Historic Landmark, this many turreted,
 completely refurbished facility offers 20,000 sq. ft. of exhibit
 space and can handle 100 8' x 10' booths and seating capacity
 for up to 2,500

Plaza Castle

A Former Police Station Now Art Museum (212) 737-7536
Boston, Massachusetts

A recycled Richardson Building, formerly a police station,
 now a museum of contemporary art in Boston's back bay
 makes available its galleries for private evening gatherings
Maximum guest capacity: 300 in galleries during the evening;
 80 in auditorium/lecture space both day and evening
Catering service

A Former Police Station Now Art Museum

A "Soho Loft"
Boston, Massachusetts

(212) 737-7536

7,000 sq. ft. of gallery space mutedly lighted by a 12' x 20'
  skylight and large arched windows. Ceiling height: 15 ft.,
  white walls, sanded wooden floors
Artwork on exhibition creates an interesting backdrop.
  Located near Federal Reserve Bank and other Boston landmarks
Maximum guest capacity: 250

A "SoHo Loft"

The Castle
Ipswich Bay, Massachusetts

(212) 737-7536

A Stuart baronial mansion designed by Chicago architect
  David Adler in 1927 during the grand era of "great houses,"
  it is surrounded by 1,352 acres of landscaped gardens and
  natural seashore. Its use for public benefits and special social
  functions as well as conferences, seminars and retreats may
  be arranged

Guest capacity: 25/30 for overnights; 300 for a wedding; 80 for
   a seminar
In-house catering service or caterer of your choice
Rental fee: $1,500 (excluding food)
Suitable for a seminar, wedding, dance, or reunion

The Castle   Photo credit: Liz Hiltunen

A Victorian Vanderbilt Estate
Asheville, North Carolina

(212) 737-7536

Beginning in 1890, a thousand workers were engaged in
   the construction of a great French Renaissance chateau
   in the Blue Ridge Mountains of North Carolina. The chateau
   was designed by architect Richard Morris Hunt for George
   Vanderbilt, grandson of Cornelius Vanderbilt. The Gardens
   and grounds were landscaped by Frederick Law Olmstead
   and Gifford Pinchot
Private parties may be arranged in a series of outbuildings which
   were also designed by Richard Morris Hunt for George Vanderbilt's
   farm operations
A gracefully designed dairy barn now offers a garden courtyard,
   a central bandstand and dance floor
Guest capacity: 600 sitdown in glass enclosed dining area
Special touches: Fresh flowers and plants from the Estate green
   houses. Blue grass bands, "clogging teams," and square dances
   may be arranged

A Victorian Vanderbilt Estate

**The Famous Newport Casino Now
  International Tennis Hall of Fame**
Newport, Rhode Island

(212) 737-7536

The Casino Building, which houses the facility, was designed
  by McKim, Mead and White for James Gordon Bennett,
  publisher of The New York Herald in 1880. The building
  complex is an outstanding example of the "Shingle" period
  of American Architecture and is on the National Register
  of Historical Buildings
Capacity of the "Trophy Room": 40-seat theatre for films and slides;
  450-seat theater for lectures, dramatic productions, etc.
Capacity of Lounge Room overlooking eight grass tennis courts: 30
Horse Shoe Piazza: 300
Ballroom: 100
Restaurant on site
Suitable for meetings, private parties, weddings, etc.

The Famous Newport Casino Now International Tennis Hall of Fame

A Summer White House
Newport, Rhode Island

(212) 737-7536

A 28 room shingle style house built in 1887. This estate,
  which was landscaped by Frederick Law Olmstead, was
  the site in 1953 of the wedding reception of Jacqueline
  Bouvier and John F. Kennedy
Indoor guest capacity (the Deck Room the Living Room
  and the Foyer): up to 150
Indoor and Outdoor guest capacity: up to 700
Suggested uses: weddings, parties, clambakes

A Summer White House

The House That Went Through Changes

The House That Went Through Changes
San Antonio, Texas
                  (212) 737-7536

Built in 1906 by architect Leo Diehlmann for Joseph Courand, Jr.,
   a grain company owner, it later became a printing shop, an
   undertaking parlor, a home for unwed mothers. Later still,
   it was occupied by the Mission Society which served the homeless.
Presently restored to its former elegance, this two-story neo-classical
   revival residence of beige brick offers verandas and porches,
   12 foot ceilings, art nouveau stained glass windows, fluted
   Corinthian columns, fireplaces and a large ballroom
Guest capacity: 500 in entire house
                60 on porches
                up to 50 in smaller rooms
Caterer on premises

The House That Was Owned By Two Presidents
Charles City County, Virginia
         (212) 737-7536

Located on the James River, this 18th century home
   is still worked as a plantation by the descendants of the
   original owners, President William Henry Harrison and
   John Tyler. This great home, which is also the largest
   framehouse in America, is typical Virginia Tidewater
   architecture and decorated with 18th century and American
   Empire motifs. It offers catered dinners, dances and cocktail
   parties under tenting. Mrs. Harrison Tyler, a descendant,
   will meet guests in person
The mansion offers formal dinners with candlelight in
   President Tyler's dining room on Tyler family silver, linen
   and porcelains. Cocktails in the Grey Room and Ball Room
The Overseers House is the 1820 home of a plantation overseer.
   One room on first floor with curving stairs leads to 2 smaller
   rooms on second floor

Guest capacity in Mansion: 18 guests with 2 members of the Tyler family and/or staff
In Overseers House: 48/60 indoor seating capacity; up to 90 for cocktails indoors and porch capacity
Under tenting on landscaped grounds: up to 800
Outside caterers may be brought in or staff of plantation will arrange entire event. Reservations required in advance for meals

The House That Was Owned by Two Presidents

Home of 35 Lees of Virginia (212) 737-7536
Alexandria, Virginia

Built by Light Horse Harry in 1785, the Lee-Fendall House has been continuously occupied by Lee family members for 188 years
Guest capacity: 100 indoors; 175 in garden with use of canopies
The garden, which features a 155-year-old magnolia tree, was designed as the town's Bicentennial Garden

Home of 35 Lees of Virginia

Renovated Grist Mill
Annandale, Virginia

(212) 737-7536

Located beside a pretty stream, 20 miles outside of Washington, D.C., this 18th century grist mill provides rustic indoor and outdoor areas for special functions. The two indoor rooms are heated and air-conditioned and have working fireplaces

Guest capacity: 140 indoors; additional guest capacity on terrace and grounds

Suggested uses: reception, banquet, party, picnic, wedding

Note: Smoking is not permitted on the premises, which are under the jurisdiction of the Fairfax County Park Authority

Renovated Grist Mill   *Photo credit: Fairfax County Park Authority*

Off the Beaten Track
Brea, California

(212) 737-7536

Nestled in a little known canyon an hour's drive from Los Angeles, where still active hot springs were discovered a century ago, this roadside lean-to hospice offers early Western ambience and a feeling of hideaway

Guest capacity: 1 to 200 indoors (with dancing); 1 to 500 outdoors

Indoor and outdoor stage for entertainment. Mountain stream. Oil derricks and orange trees down the road

Suggested uses: weddings and private celebrations, company parties, motion picture location shooting

Off the Beaten Track

* * * * * * *

ADDENDA:

City Gallery
2 Columbus Circle
New York, N.Y. 10019
Contact: Ellen Liman, Director

Curated exhibit space to non-profit organizations in
   New York City
20' x 75' of space is available with 15' ceilings
Rental fee: none
Professional lighting, temperature controlled
Note: Request for guidelines must be made in writing. This
   space has only recently been made available in what was
   the Huntington Hartford Museum

An Indoor Vest-Pocket Park with Waterfall   737-7536
New York, N.Y.

Guest capacity: Potentially very large. Exact figure
   not available at time of printing
Caterer on premises

A Penthouse in Rockefeller Center   737-7536
New York, N.Y.

Guest capacity: 500 sitdown
                1000 cocktails
Smaller rooms available as well
Caterer on premises

Photographer's Loft with Parquet Floors   737-7536
(near Gramercy Park)
New York, N.Y.

2nd floor loft space
Seating capacity: approximately 100 classroom style/
   200 for cocktails
12' ceilings, many windows, bar, kitchen; food may be served
Suggested uses: meeting dance, party, location shooting, etc.

3,000 sq. ft. Loft on West 27th Street   737-7536
New York, N.Y.

2 rooms make up this loft space on the 7th floor
Seating capacity: 300 people may be accommodated in
   3,000 sq. ft. of space
Rental fee: approximately $600
Non-working fireplace, 1907 pool table, elevator, ceiling fans
   on 12 ft. ceilings, bay window with southern exposure, part
   antique/part high-tech decor, kitchen; food may be served
Suggested uses: private party, fashion shooting

A Victorian Mansion and Growth Center
Yonkers, N.Y.

(212) 737-7536

Several living-room style rooms available for consciousness raising and growth workshops in large Victorian mansion overlooking Hudson River.
Guest capacity: approximately 15 in each room
Vegetarian catering on premises

Westchester Lighthouse
346 Mamaroneck Avenue
White Plains, N.Y. 10605

(914) 761-3221

Meeting room
Seating capacity: 20/50
Rental fee: none
Kitchen; refreshments may be served
Note: Space is only available to non-profit groups

A Richardsonian House
St. Louis, Missouri

(212) 737-7536

A 42-room Romanesque mansion designed by the architect Thomas Annon, who was greatly influenced by Harry A. Richardson. Built for a 19th century self-made businessman who dealt in woodware, this house, its 20 fireplaces, magnificent woodcarvings, iron work and stained glass cost $500,000 in 1890 currency. Presently owned by St. Louis University, its rooms decorated with restored period furniture are open to the public.
Guest capacity: 150 sitdown; 200 cocktails
Caterer on premises

A Richardsonian House

INDEX

A

Aaron Davis Hall, 6, *119*
Abraham Goodman House, 42, *88*, 114
Abundance, *140*
Academic Review, 69, *71*
Actor's Playhouse, 42, *95*, 114
Actors Repertory Theatre, *95*, 114
Adelphi Academy, 42, *123*
Alice Tully Hall, 6, *88*
All Saint's Church, *28*, 42
Alley Park, *85*
Alum Dance Studio, *114*
Ambrose Lightship, *12*
American Academy and Institute of Arts and Letters, 6, 7, 114
American Arbitration Association, 69, *71*
The American Association of University Women, 69, *71*, 114
The American Mime Theatre, *95*, 114
American Museum of Natural History, *154*
American Place Theater, 42, *97*
American Standard Exhibition Center, 42, *44*
American Theatre of Actors, *97*
Ansonia Hotel, *53*, 114
Anthroposophical Society of America, 69, *71*, 114
Appel Farm Arts and Music Center, *29*, 42
Arden House, *29*
Armories, *5*, 42
Art on the Beach, *85*
Art Carnival at Lincoln Center, *49*
Art Deco Nightclub, *37*
Artists Space, 42, *45*
Asphalt Green Youth, Sports and Arts Center, *39*
Association of Artist-Run Galleries, Inc., 42, *97*
Auditoriums, *6*, 69
Automat, America's Only, *154*
Avant-garde Art Gallery, *65*
Avery Fisher Hall, 7, *88*, 155

B

Balloons, *12*
The Ballroom at the Windows on the World, *10*
Ballrooms, *10*
Bandshells, *94*
Banquet Facility, *170*
The Barbizon, *42*
The Barbizon Hotel, *53*, 114
The Barbizon Plaza Hotel, 6, 42, *54*
Bard College, 42, *125*
Bard Hall, 42, 69, *71*
Bardavon 1869 Opera House, *88*
Bargemusic, Ltd., *14*
Barges, *12*
Baronial Mansion, A, Reborn, *140*
The Beacon Theater, 6, 42, *97*, 114
Bear Mountain Inn, *30*
Beaten Path, *112*
Beaten Path, Off the, *196*
Bentley's, *35*
Berkshire Place, *54*
Bethune Senior Center, *85*
Birthday Room, *176*
Blackwell House, *155*
Bloomingdale House of Music, 42, *90*
Boats, *12*
Books and Company, *113*
Borough of Manhattan Community College, *117*
Bouwerie Lane Theatre, *98*, 114
Branch Brook Skating Center, *128*
Brandi, *35*

Bring Sailing Back, Inc., *14*
Bronx Community College, *122*
Bronx High School of Science, *6*
Bronx House, *72*, 114
The Bronx Museum of the Arts, 42, *45*
Brooklyn Academy of Music, 6, *90*
Brooklyn Botanic Garden, 69, *155*
Brooklyn Botanic Garden Fence Art Show, *49*
Brooklyn College, *90*
Brooklyn Museum, 42, *45*
Brooklyn YWCA, 6, 42, *134*
Brookville Park, *85*
The Buckley School, 42, 114, *117*
Burlington House, *86*

C

The Cabaret, *14*
Calderone Concert Hall, 6, 42, *90*
Cami Hall, 42, *90*, 114
Canarsie Pier–Gateway National Recreation Area, *41*
Capital Children's Museum, *177*
Caranci Studios, *98*, 114
Carnegie Conference Center, *30*
Carnegie Hall Corporation, The, *91*, 114
Carnegie Recital Hall, *91*, 114
Carousels, *174*
Carter Theatre, *98*, 114
The Casino, Famous Newport, *192*
Castle, The, *191*
Cathedral Church of St. John the Divine, *19*, 42
Cathedral of St. James, The, *25*, 42
Catholic Kolping Society, 69, *72*
Caumsett Mansion, *39*
Center for Inter-American Relations, 69, *72*
Central Park Mall, *94*
Central Park Outdoor Art Exhibit, *49*
Central Queens YMCA, 42, *135*
Central Synagogue, *19*, 42
Charas/New Assembly Performance Space, *98*
Charles Green Center, *113*
Chase Manhattan Plaza, *86*
Chelsea Hall, *114*
Chelsea Theatre Center, *109*
"Choreoground" and Dance Studios, *114*
Christ and St. Stephen's Church, *19*
Christ United Methodist Church, *28*
Church Center for the U.N., *20*, 42
Church of St. Ann and The Holy Trinity, *25*
Church of the Covenant, *20*, 42
Churches, *19*
Church Within, The, *20*
Circle in the Square, 6, *98*, *99*, 114
Circle Line Sightseeing Yachts, *14*
City Center 55th Street Theater, 7, 42, *99*, 114
City College of CUNY, 6, *119*
City Gallery, *197*
Clark Center for the Performing Arts, *114*
Clock Towers, *48*
Clove Lakes Park, *85*
Coach House/Stable, An 18th Century, *156*
Coco's Disco Rink, *115*
Colden Auditorium/Queens College, *6*
Coliseum, The, *128*
College of Mt. St. Vincent, 6, *30*
College of Staten Island, The, 6, *125*
Colleges, *117*

199

Colonial Park, *94*
Colonnades Theatre Lab, Inc., 42, *99,* 114
Columbia University, 6, 10, *119*
Columbia University Teachers College, *6*
Columbia Yacht, *15*
Community Church of New York, The, 6, *20*
Community Gallery, Brooklyn Museum, 42, *45*
Concord Baptist Church, The, 6, *26,* 42
Conference Centers, *29*
Conference Rooms, *69*
Congregation B'nai Jeshurun, 6, 10, *20,* 42
Congregation B'nai Sholom, *26,* 42
Congregational Church of North New York, 6, *25,* 42
Cooking Center in the W. 30's, 69, *72*
Co-operative Auditorium, 6, *7*
Cooper Union Great Hall, *120*
Copacabana, *35*
Creative Space Near Central Park, *140*
Crotona Park, *83*
Crystal Palace, *10*
Cultural Affairs Department, 42, 69, *73*
Cunningham Park, *85*
C.W. Post Center of Long Island University, 42, 114, *123*

D

Dairy, The, *156*
Dalton School, The, *120*
Damrosch Park, *94*
Dance Theater Workshop, Inc., *99,* 114
Deerpark Farms Resort, *30*
Dennis Wayne Dancer's School, 42, *100,* 114
Department of Cultural Affairs, 42, 69, *73*
Department of General Services, *131*
De Seversky Conference Center, *131*
Designer Loft in SoHo, *141*
Diners, Streamlined Railroad, *146*
Diocese of the Armenian Church of America, 6, *21,* 42
Discos, *35*
District 1199, 6, *7,* 10, 42, 69
Division of Real Property, *131*
Donnell Library Center, 42, *100*
John J. Downing Stadium, *128*
Dramatis Personae, 42, *99,* 114
Drawing Center, The, *65*
Drew Hamilton C.Y.O. Community Center, 42, *69,* 114

E

Ear Inn, *113*
Earl Hall Center, 10, *119*
East Flatbush Rugby Y, 42, *134*
East River Park, *94*
East River Savings Bank, 42, *45*
East 63rd Street Townhouse Floor, *142*
East Side International Community Center, Inc., 69, *73,* 114
East/West Center, *42*
East/West Center for Holistic Health, 69, *73*
Eastern Christian Leasing Center, 6, *9,* 42, 69, 114
Edgar Alien Poe Festival, *52*
Edison Theater, 6, *100,* 114
Educational Alliance, Inc., 6, *9,* 42, 69, 114
88 Pine Street Plaza, *86*
18th Century Stone Coach House/Stable, Now Museum, An, *156*
1828 Quaker Meeting House, *170*
Eleanora, *127*
Electric Circus Disco/Club, *37,* 42
Elegant "French Bistro" Loft, *142*
Eltingville Lutheran School, *125*
Empire Roller Disco, *115*
Empire Rollerdome, *115*
English Country Estate/Conference Center, *150*
Enid A. Haupt Conservatory/New York Botanical Garden, *160*
Entermedia Theater, 6, 42, *100,* 114
Environmental Centers, *39*

Equitable Gallery, 42, *46*
Eric, *113*
Essex County Department of Parks, Recreation and Cultural Affairs, *128*
Ethical Humanist Society of Long Island, *42*
Exhibition/Hospitality Railroad Car, 42, *46,* 69
Exhibitions, *42*
Experimental Theatre, The, *119*
Expositions, *42*

F

Faculty House, 69, *73,* 142
Fairgrounds, *50*
Fairleigh Dickinson University, *126*
Fashion Industry High School, *7*
Fashion Institute of Technology, 6, 42, 114, *120*
Fashion Moda, *113*
Feast of Saint Anthony, *52*
Feast of San Genaro, *52*
Ferris Booth Hall/Columbia University, 6, *119*
Fifth Avenue Hotel, 42, *54,* 114
Fifth Avenue Loft with a Tree-top View of Historic Park, *67*
52nd Street Fair, The, *52*
Fin de Siecle Intimacy in Spacious Interior, *143*
Fireboathouse Conference Center, *41*
Five Towns Music and Art Foundation, *91*
Flea Market Locations, *50*
Floyd Bennett Field—Gateway National Recreation Area, *41,* 42
Flushing Jewish Center, 6, 10, 42, 69, *74,* 114
Flushing Meadows—Corona Park, *85*
Forest Park, *85,* 94
Former Greenhouse/Now Restaurant, *158*
Former Union Hall and Neighborhood Bar/Now Irish Pub, *158*
Fort Hancock-Gateway National Recreation Area, *41*
Fort Hancock Post Theatre—Gateway National Recreation Area, *41*
42nd Street Theatre Row, Inc., *100,* 114
Foundation for the Advance of Dance, *101,* 114
Franz Siegel Park, *94*
Fraunces Tavern Museum, 42, 69, *74*
Frederick Douglass Community Center, 69, *74*
French Country Loft, *179*
Frost Valley YMCA, *31*

G

Galeria Morivivi, *113*
Gallery Theater, *113*
Garden District Mansion, A, *188*
Gateway National Recreation Area, *41,* 42, 69
Gene Frankl Theatre Workshop, Inc., *101,* 114
George Morrison Studios, 69, *74,* 114
Georgian Suite, *143*
Gershwin Hall, *6*
Giant Stadium, *129*
Gimbel's East, 42, 69, *74*
Golden Gate Motor Inn, *54*
Good Neighbor Church, *21*
Good Shepherd-Faith Presbyterian Church, *21*
The Goodskates, *115*
A Graceful Inn/Conference Center, *31*
Gracie Square Art Exhibit, *49*
Gracious Murray Hill Brownstone, *143*
Gramercy Arts Theater, *101*
Grand Central Station, *157*
Grand Hyatt New York, *55*
Greenhouse/Now Restaurant, Former, *158*
Greenwich House Music School, 42, *91,* 114
Grist Mill, Renovated, *196*
Grolier Club, 42, *46*
The Solomon Guggenheim Museum, *91,* 113
Guild Rehearsal Studios, *101,* 114
Gulbenkian Cultural Center, *42*
Gustave Hartman YM-YWHA, 42, 114, *135*
Gymnasiums, see Schools, *117*

H

Haffen Park, *94*
Halloran House, *55*
Hammarskjold Plaza, 42, *86*
Hampton Roads, *183*
Harkness House, 10, 69, 114, *143*
Harlem State Office Building, 42, 69, 75
Harlequin Rehearsal Studio, *101,* 114
The Harley of New York, *55*
Harrison House Conference Center, *32*
Hartley House, 69, 75
Haut Voyage Balloons, Inc., *15*
Hayden Planetarium, *158*
Helen Carey Playhouse, Brooklyn Academy of Music, *6*
The Henry Chauncey Conference Center, *32*
High School of Art and Design, *6*
Hilltop Hudson Valley Mansion, *150*
Hofstra University, 6, *124*
Holiday Hills, *32*
Holiday Inn, 6, *55*
Home of 35 Lees of Virginia, *195*
Homey Loft in Tribeca, A, *67*
Hominy Hill Golf Course, *33*
Horace Mann Auditorium, 6, *119*
Hotel Algonquin, *53*
Hotel Overlooking Gramercy Park, 42, *56,* 114
Hotel Plaza, *56*
Hotels, *53*
House on Library Plaza, The, *151*
House That Was Owned by 2 Presidents, The, *194*
House That Went Through Changes, The, *194*
Hudson Guild, 42, 69, 75, 114
Hudson Valley Wine Co., Inc., *171*
Hughes Hall, 69, 75
Hunter College Concert Bureau, 6, *101*
Hunter Island, *83*
Hunts Point Palace, 6, *10*

I

The Ice Studio, *115*
Institute for Art & Urban Resources/Project Studios One (P.S. 1), 44, *48, 131*
Interferon Nightclub, *37*
Inter-Media Art Center, Inc., *132*
International House, 6, *44,* 114
International Hospitality Suite, *158*
Iona College, 7, *44, 124*
The Irish Arts Center, *102,* 114
Italian Renaissance Villa and Gardens, *184*

J

Jacob Riis Houses Amphitheater, 6, *102*
Jail, An Old County Courthouse and, *186*
Jamaica Arts Center, 44, *132*
James Weldon Johnson Community Centers, Inc., 6, 44, *102,* 114
Jazz, see John Andrew Spaulding's Jazz Gallery, *69*
Jazz Loft on West 27th Street, *67*
Jewish Center of Bayside Hills, 10, 44, 69, 75
Jewish Community Center of Yonkers, 69, *76*
Jewish Guild for the Blind, 69, *76*
The Jewish Museum, 44, 69, *76*
John Andrew Spaulding's Jazz Gallery, *69*
Julia Richmond High School, *6*
Justine, *37*

K

K & K Space and Toy Co., Inc., *67,* 114
Kingsland Homestead, *158*
Know How Workshop, *102*

L

LaGuardia Community College, 44, 114, *124*
La Guardia Memorial House, 6, *9,* 44, 69
Langston Hughes Community Library and Cultural Center, 44, 69, *76*
Large Art Deco Nightclub/Entertainment Complex, *37*
Le Figaro Cafe, *113*
Lehman College Center for Performing Arts, 6, 44, *92,* 114, *122*
Lenox Hill Neighborhood Association, 69, *76*
Leperq Space/Brooklyn Academy of Music, *6*
Leviticus International Entertainment Complex, *38*
Libraries, *59-65*
Library/Cultural Center, *185*
Library and Museum of the Performing Arts, 44, *92, 159*
Library Plaza, The House on, *151*
Lighthouse, Westchester, *197*
Light Opera of Manhattan, 44, *102*
Lincoln Center Plazas, *86*
Lincoln Center Plaza Arts and Crafts Exhibits, *49*
Lockwood-Mathews Mansion, *137*
Loeb Student Center, 44, 114, *121*
Loft of a Caterer and an Indoor Landscaper, Living, *144*
Loft, Elegant "French Bistro", *142*
Loft, A Homey in Tribeca, *67*
Loft, Movie-Set, *144*
Loft with Parquet Floors, Photographer's, *196*
Loft for Musical Functions, A, *67*
Loft with Roof Terrace, Studio, *147*
Loft, A "SoHo", *191*
Loft in SoHo, Designer, *141*
Loft, 3,000 Sq. Ft. on West 27th Street, *197*
Loft with Three Skylights, *67*
Lofts, *65*
Long Island Ferry Boat, *15*
Long Island University, 6, 44, 114, *123*
Lutheran Church of the Risen Christ, *26,* 44
Lyndhurst, *171*

M

Madison Avenue Baptist Church, *21,* 44
Madison Square Garden Center, 44, *129*
Magno Park Avenue Screening Room, *127*
Magno Penthouse Screening Room, *127*
Magno Preview, *127*
Magno Sound and Video, *127*
Manhattan Beach Park, *83*
Manhattan Church of the Nazarene, 10, *22*
Manhattan Punch Line Theatre, 44, *103,* 114
Manhattan School of Music, 6, *92,* 114
Manhattan Theater Club, *103,* 114
Manhattanville College, 10, *126*
Manhattanville Community Centers, Inc., 69, 77, 114
Mansion, A Garden District, *188*
Mansion of the First Commander of the USS Enterprise, *190*
Mansion and Growth Center, A Victorian, *198*
Mansion Which Was Built by a Wagon-Builder Named Studebaker, *187*
Marc Ballroom, 6, *10,* 114
Marcus Garvey Park, *94*
Marion Castle, *180*
Martin Luther King Junior High School, *6*
Marymount College, *126*
Marymount Manhattan College, 6, 10, 44, 114, *120*
McMillan Theater, 6, *119*
Mechanics Institute, 69, 77
Meeting Rooms, *69*
Mercantile Library Association, 69, 77
Merce Cunningham Studio, *103,* 114
Metropolis Roller Skate Club, 44, 69, *116*
Metropolitan Museum of Art, *159*
Metropolitan Opera Association, 7, *92, 159*
Metropolitan Republican Club, 44, 69, 77, 114
Millbank Chapel, Columbia University, *119*
Mini-Parks, *85*
Sam & Esther Minskoff Cultural Center, 10, 44, 69, *78,* 114

The Mon Lei, *16*
Morris-Jumel Mansion, 69, *159*
Morse Mime Theater, 44, *103*, 114
Mosholu-Montefiore Community Center, 44, 69, 78, 114
Mostly Magic, *177*
Movie-Set Loft, *144*
Mule Barge, Old Fashioned, *16*
Multi-Media Party Space in the West 80's, *38*
Multi-Use of Public School Buildings, *132*
Murray Hill Townhouse, *145*
The Museum of Broadcasting, 69, *78*
Museum of the City of New York, *177*
Museum of Holography, 44, *160*
Museum House, A, *179*
Museum on the Hudson River, *172*
Museum Mile, *52*
Museum with Japanese Stroll Gardens, *172*
Museum, Ship, *185*

N

The Nameless Theatre, *103*, 114
Napa Valley Winery, *182*
Nassau Veterans Memorial Coliseum, 44, *129*
Nat Horne Theatre, *104*, 114
The Nazarene Congregational United Church of Christ, *26*
New Dramatists, Inc., *104*, 114
Newfoundland, *104*, 113, 114
The New Lincoln School, 114, *121*
New York Academy of Sciences, 10, 44, 69, *78*
New York Blood Center, 69, *78*
New York Botanical Garden, *159*, *161*
New York Chamber of Commerce & Industry, *161*
New York City Department of Marine & Aviation, *16*
New York City Department of Ports & Terminals, *110*
New York City Mission Society, Mission Town House, 6, *104*
New York City Passenger Ship Terminal—Pier No. 92, 6, 44, *112*
New York Coliseum, 44, *46*
New York Experience Theater, *162*
New York Exposition & Convention Center, 44, 47, *162*
New York Genealogical & Biographical Society, 69, *79*
New York New York Disco & Restaurant, *38*
The New York Public Library, *59*, *162*
New York Public Transit Exhibit, 44, *163*
New York School of Printing, 6, *121*
New York Society for Ethical Culture, 6, *22*
New York Society for the New Church, *22*, 44
New York State Theater, *6*
New York University, 44, 114, *121*
Nightclub, Large Art Deco, *37*
Ninth Avenue Fair, *53*
92nd Street YM-YWHA, 6, *133*
No Smoking Playhouse, *104*
Nola Sound Studios, Inc., *105*, 114
Norman Thomas High School, *6*
North Shore Gold Coast Mansion, *174*
Nostalgia Special, *164*

O

Off the Beaten Track, *196*
Off Center Theatre, *105*, 114
Ohio, *113*
Old County Courthouse and Jail, An, *186*
Old Fashioned Mule Barges, *16*
Old Merchant's House, *169*
One Astor Place, *105*, 114
112 Workshop, Inc., *44*
One World Festival, *52*
127 John Street, *87*
The Open Eye, *105*
Orchard Beach, *83*
Organization of Independent Artists, *133*
The Oval Room, 44, 69, *79*
Oyster Bay and Crystal Palace, *10*

P

Pace University, 6, *121*
The Palace, *57*
The Palladium, 7, 44, *105*, 114
Park Circle Roller Skating Rink, 44, 114, *116*
Park with Waterfall, An Indoor Vest-Pocket, *197*
Parker Meridien New York, *57*
Parks, *83*
Parsons School of Design, 44, *121*
Party Places, *140*
Party Space in the West 80's, *38*
Path, 44, *47*
Peking, *17*
Pelham Bay Park, *83*
Penthouse in Rockefeller Center, A, *197*
People's Institutional A.M.E. Church, 6, *26*, 44
Performance Spaces, *88-110*
Permits, *52*
Phillips Fine Art Auctioneers, *164*
Phipps Central Harlem Center, 69, *79*
Photographer's Loft with Parquet Floors, *197*
Picnic Areas, *83*
Pier 16, *112*
Pier 83, *14*
Pier 84, *110*
Pier 92, 6, 44, *112*
Piers, *110*; see New York City Passenger Ship Terminal, Pier No. 92, 6, 44, *112*
Pioneer, *17*, 44
Pippin's, *38*
Plantation House on the Banks of the Mississippi, The South's Largest, *189*
Plantation with 250 Year Old Oak Trees, The, *188*
Playhouse 46, *22*
Plaza Castle, A Former Armory Now Meeting and Exhibit Space, *190*
Plazas, *85*
Poe Park, *94*
Poetry Reading Places, *112*
Poetry at St. Clement's, *113*
Police Station Now Art Museum, A Former, *190*
Postgraduate Center West, *10*
Pratt Institute, 7, 44, 47, 114
Prince of Peace Moravian Church, *28*
Private Club Overlooking a Private Park, A, *144*
Private Floor with Entertainment, A, *165*
Private Party Places, Nationwide, *182*
Private School Near New York City, Spacious, *151*
The Production Company, *106*, 114
Project Studios One, 44, *48*, *131*
Promenade and Fine Arts Exhibition, *49*
Prospect Park, *83*, 94
P.S. 1, 44, *48*, *131*
Pub, Irish, *158*
Public School Buildings, Multi-use of, *121-22*, *132*
The Purple Barge, *17*

Q

Quaker Meeting House, 1828, *170*
Queen Anne Style Mansion, A, *183*
Queensborough Community College, 6, 44, 114, *124*
Queens Botanical Garden, *165*
Queens College, *92*, *124*
Queens College/Colden Auditorium, *6*
Queens College Student Union, 6, 10, 44, *124*
Queens College Theater, *6*
The Queens Museum, 44, 69, *79*

R

Racquet Club in Yorkville, *145*
Radio City Music Hall, 7, 44, *93*, 114, *165*
Recently Restored Landmark Hotel, 44, *57*
Red Brick Federal Style Townhouse, *146*

Reflections, *38*
Reformed Church of Staten Island, 6, *28*
Regine's, *39*
Rehearsal Places, *114*
Restored Village, 44, 69, *166*
Rice Playfield, *83*
Rice Stadium, *130*
Richard Allen Center for Culture & Art, 44, *106*
Larry Richardson's Dance Gallery, *106*
Rinks, *115*
Riverdale Country School, 114, *123*
Riverdale-Yonkers Society for Ethical Culture, 44, 69, 79, *114*
Rizzoli Editore Corporation, *128*
Roberto Clemente State Park, 6, 44, 87, *114*
Rockaway Beach, *85*
Rogers Locomotive Works, *138*
"The Room" on West 13th Street, *146*
Roosevelt Hotel, *54*
Roseland, 7, 10, *44*
The Roxy, *116*
Rumpelmayer's Restaurant, *177*

S

Salem Community Service Council, Inc., *24*, 69
Sandy Hook Unit–Gateway National Recreation Area, *41*
Margaret Sanger Center, 69, *77*
St. Clement's Church, *22*, 113
St. Clement's Theatre, *22*
St. George Campus/College of Staten Island, *125*
St. Hilda's & St. Hugh's Church, 6, 44, 114, *122*
St. John the Divine, *19*
St. John's Church Parish Hall, *29*, 44
St. John's Episcopal Church, *27*, 44
St. John's Hall, 10, *23*, 44
St. John-St. Matthew Emmanuel Community Center, *27*
St. John's University, 44, *47*
St. Mark's Church-in-the-Bowery, 6, *23*, 113
St. Mary's Manhattanville Episcopal Church, *44*
St. Paul's Chapel/Columbia University, 6, *120*
St. Peter's Church, 6, *23*, 44
St. Peter's Episcopal Church, *44*
St. Phillip's Community Service Council, Inc., *23*, 44
St. Regis Penthouse, *58*
St. Regis Roof, *58*
St. Regis-Sheraton, *58*
St. Thomas Church, *24*
Savoy Manor, *9*
School of International Affairs Auditorium, *120*
Schools, *117*
Screening Rooms, *127*
Seamen's Church Institute of New York, 10, 44, 69, *80*
Seaside Park, *94*
Seven Springs Center, *34*
77 Water Street, *87*
78th Street Theatre Lab, *106*
Shadow Lawn, *137*
Allen Shandler Recreation Area, *83*
Shea Municipal Stadium, *130*
Sheraton Center, 10, *58*
Ship Museum, *184*
Sky Rink, 69, *117*
Sloane House YMCA, 44, 114, *134*
Sniffen Court, *180*
Snuff Mill Restaurant/N.Y. Botanical Garden, *161*
Snug Harbor Cultural Center, 6, 44, *166*
William Sobelsohn Associates, 69, *80*
Society for the Advancement of Judaism, *114*
"SoHo Loft", A, *191*
SoHo Repertory Theatre, *107*
South Beach, *85*
South Mountain Arena, *129*
South Street Seaport, *167*
Spacious Private School Near New York City, *151*
Spanish Theater Repertory Co., Ltd., *107*
John Andrew Spaulding's Jazz Gallery, 69, *92*

Stadiums, *128*
Staten Island Ferry, 6, *16*
Steps, *130*
Sterling Forest Conference Center, *34*
Streamlined Railroad Diners, *145*
Street Activity Permit, *52*
Street Fairs, *50*
Studebaker, The Mansion Which Was Built By a Wagon-Builder Named, *186*
Studio of Creative Movement, *68*, 114
Studio 505, *68*
Studio Loft with Roof Terrace, *147*
Studio Spaces, *131*
Studio We, *68*
Studios 58 Playhouse, Inc., 44, 69, 80, *114*
Stuyvesant High School, *6*
Subway Mezzanines as Exhibit Places, *44*
Subways, see Nostalgia Special, *163*
Summer White House, A, *192*
Supperclubs, *35*
Sutton Gym, *176*
Sutton Place Synagogue, 6, 10, *24*
Symphony Space, Inc., 6, *93*, 114

T

TAMA County Fair, *52*
Tarrytown House, *34*
Temple Isaiah, 10, *27*
Tennis Hall of Fame, Newport Casino, Now, *193*
Terrace on the Park, 6, 10, *44*
Thalia Spanish Theatre, *107*
Theater De Lys, *107*
Theatre, Opera, Music Institute, Inc., *107*
Third Avenue Fair, *52*
Third Street Music School Settlement, *93*, 114
Thirteenth Street Theatre, 44, *108*, 114, 178
The Tibet Center, 69, *80*
George Tomov Studio, 69, *74*, 114
Tompkins Square Park, *94*
Town Hall, 6, *93*
Townhouse Floor on East 63rd Street, *142*
Townhouse, Murray Hill, *143*
Townhouse, Red Brick Federal Style, *146*
Truman High School, *6*
Turtle Bay Music School, *93*
Twin Island, *83*

U

Union Hall, Former, *158*
Union Square Theatre, 44, *108*, 114
Uniquely Private Setting, A, *147*
United Methodist Parish in Bushwick, 6, *27*
United Nations, The, *166*
United Nations Plaza Hotel, The, 44, *58*
Universalist Church of New York, 6, *24*
Upper Eastside Street Fair, *52*
Urban Mansion with Windows Facing Inward, An, *186*
U.S. Custom House, *168*
U.S. Tennis Association National Tennis Center, *130*
USS Ling, The, *178*

V

Van Cortlandt Park, *83*
Van Cortlandt Park Stadium, 7, *130*
Vandam Theater, SoHo, 44, *108*, 114
Vanderbilt Estate, A Victorian, *192*
Vanderbilt YMCA, *134*
Versatile Dance/Rehearsal Loft on W. 21st Street, 68, *114*
Victorian Mansion and Growth Center, A, *198*
Victorian Mansion/Now Private School, *151*
Villa Which Was Built For a Saloonkeeper, *182*
Village Community School, *122*
Village Gate, *109*

Village Halloween Parade, *52*
Village Skating, *117*
Vista International Hotel, *58*
Vital Arts Center, *109*, 114

W

Wagner College, 6, 44, *125*
Wagner Junior High School, *6*
Wainwright House, *173*
Ward-Nasse Gallery, *109*, 114
Ward's Island, *83*
Washington Irving High School, *6*
Washington Square Church, *25*
Washington Square Outdoor Art Show, *49*
Waterfall, Indoor Vest-Pocket Park with, An, *197*
Water Mill, A White-washed Room in a, *152*
Waterside Swim and Health Club, 69, *81*
Wave Hill Center for Environmental Studies, *41*, 44, 69, *168*
Wayside Cottage, *175*
Westchester Lighthouse, *198*
Westside Arts Theatre, *109*
The Westside Mainstage, *109*
Westside YMCA, *134*
White Columns, *47*
White House, A Summer, *193*
White Mask Theatre Corporation, 44, *110*, 114
White-washed Room in a Water Mill, A, *152*
Whitman Hall/Brooklyn College, *6*
William Paterson College Student Center, 10, *127*
Willowbrook Park, *85*
Willkie Memorial Building, 44, 69, *80*
Winery, Napa Valley, *182*
Wolfe's Pond Park, *85*
Womanbooks, *113*
Women's City Club of New York, Inc., 69, *81*
Workmen's Circle Building, 10, 44, 69, *81*, 114
The World Trade Center, 44, *45*, *48*, *87*
World Trade Center Terminal, 44, *47*
WPA Theater, *109*, 114
The Writer's Room, *133*

X

Xenon, *39*

Y

Y's, *133*
Yankee Stadium, *130*
YM-YWHA of Greater Flushing, *135*
YM & YWHA of Williamsburg, Inc., *44*
York Preparatory School, *122*
Young Men's Christian Association, McBurney Branch, 44, *134*